Also available from ASQ Quality Press:

The Quality Toolbox, Second Edition
Nancy R. Tague

The Quality Improvement Handbook, Second Edition
ASQ Quality Management Division and John E. Bauer, Grace L. Duffy,
Russell T. Westcott, editors

The Certified Manager of Quality/Organizational Excellence Handbook, Third Edition
Russell T. Westcott, editor

Bringing Business Ethics to Life: Achieving Corporate Social Responsibility
Bjørn Andersen

Correct! Prevent! Improve!: Driving Improvement Through Problem Solving and Corrective and Preventive Action
Jeanne Ketola and Kathy Roberts

Quality Essentials: A Reference Guide from A to Z
Jack B. ReVelle

Failure Mode and Effect Analysis: FMEA from Theory to Execution, Second Edition
D. H. Stamatis

Business Performance Through Lean Six Sigma: Linking the Knowledge Worker, the Twelve Pillars, and Baldrige
James T. Schutta

Business Process Improvement Toolbox
Bjørn Andersen

Performance Measurement Explained: Designing and Implementing Your State-of-the-Art System
Bjørn Andersen and Tom Fagerhaug

The Path to Profitable Measures: 10 Steps to Feedback That Fuels Performance
Mark W. Morgan

To request a complimentary catalog of ASQ Quality Press publications, call 800-248-1946, or visit our Web site at http://qualitypress.asq.org.

Root Cause Analysis

Root Cause Analysis

Simplified Tools and Techniques

Second Edition

Bjørn Andersen
Tom Fagerhaug

ASQ Quality Press
Milwaukee, Wisconsin

American Society for Quality, Quality Press, Milwaukee 53203
© 2006 by ASQ
All rights reserved. Published 2006
Printed in the United States of America
12 11 10 09   5 4

Library of Congress Cataloging-in-Publication Data

Andersen, Bjørn.
    Root cause analysis : simplified tools and techniques / Bjørn Andersen, Tom Fagerhaug.
        p. cm.
    Includes bibliographical references and index.
    ISBN-13: 978-0-87389-692-4 (soft cover : alk. paper)
    ISBN-10: 0-87389-692-0 (soft cover : alk. paper)
    1. Total quality management. 2. Problem solving. 3. Quality control. I. Fagerhaug, Tom, 1968–
II. Title.

    HD62.15.A53 2006
    658.4'013—dc22   2006013169

ISBN-13: 978-0-87389-692-4
ISBN-10: 0-87389-692-0

Publisher: William A. Tony
Acquisitions Editor: Annemieke Hytinen
Project Editor: Paul O'Mara
Production Administrator: Randall Benson

ASQ Mission: The American Society for Quality advances individual, organizational, and community excellence worldwide through learning, quality improvement, and knowledge exchange.

Attention Bookstores, Wholesalers, Schools and Corporations: ASQ Quality Press books, videotapes, audiotapes, and software are available at quantity discounts with bulk purchases for business, educational, or instructional use. For information, please contact ASQ Quality Press at 800-248-1946, or write to ASQ Quality Press, P.O. Box 3005, Milwaukee, WI 53201-3005.

To place orders or to request a free copy of the ASQ Quality Press Publications Catalog, including ASQ membership information, call 800-248-1946. Visit our Web site at www.asq.org or http://qualitypress.asq.org.

Printed in the United States of America

 Printed on acid-free paper

 Quality Press
600 N. Plankinton Avenue
Milwaukee, Wisconsin 53203
Call toll free 800-248-1946
Fax 414-272-1734
www.asq.org
http://qualitypress.asq.org
http://standardsgroup.asq.org
E-mail: authors@asq.org

Table of Contents

Preface to the
Second Edition

We finished the manuscript for the first edition of this book in the fall of 1999, more than seven years from the date of this preface for the second edition. Since then, we have been truly amazed by the response to the book. We had been asked by ASQ Quality Press whether we would consider writing a book on the topic of root cause analysis, so this was really not our idea to begin with. Having worked in the field of quality management, improvement work, and general problem solving for many years by that time, we quickly warmed to the idea. Some research into the existing literature quickly demonstrated that very little authoritative information was available and that root cause analysis was in no way a well-defined, singular concept. So we got started on outlining a structure for a book, very early on deciding to make it a book for practitioners at any level in any organization.

Since its publication, *Root Cause Analysis: Simplified Tools and Techniques* has sold more than 10,000 copies, a figure we would not have imagined in our wildest dreams when making the finishing touches to the manuscript in September 1999. Even more gratifying are the many responses received from readers, telling us how they have used the book and the tools explained in it to solve a diverse set of problems. Both the sales figures and these responses confirmed our assessment that there was indeed something missing in the literature to be found at the time, and that an easy-to-read, practically oriented book of this type was needed to fill this gap.

However, seven years is a long time in the world of quality. New techniques evolve, people, organizations, or researchers tweak tools and techniques to come up with new applications, and we all grow a little wiser. Looking at the book now, it is clear to us that the first edition stopped a little too abruptly: we only got as far as identifying the root cause of a problem, and that is really only halfway to where we need to go. The root cause must be eliminated by finding a new solution, and the new solution must be implemented and proven to work. Remarks from readers confirmed our suspicions, some even asking us how to proceed with their problem after having found the root cause.

After seeing how people used the book, we also noticed that the templates provided throughout the book were only somewhat helpful in that they might provide a head start in using a certain tool but having to copy the templates from the actual book, with the very limited possibilities for scaling or editing, was not very user-friendly. Including these on a CD-ROM thus seemed another obvious improvement to the book. These improvements, combined with reworking the chapter structure to make it adhere more closely to the overall problem solving process, as well as adding an occasional tool or example here and there, would help the book take a leap into the next millennium.

The idea was put to ASQ Quality Press, they mulled it over, and with encouragement from external reviewers it was agreed that the idea was indeed a good one. As a result, we have now spent some months updating the book to make it an even more useful tool than the first edition. We can only hope that our readers appreciate the effort (or tell us if not so that we can improve it further in another seven years!).

As in the preface to the first edition, we provide you with some instructions on the use of the book. Root cause analysis is best suited for the frontline employee and is not reserved for the organization's quality manager. It is most effective when applied by groups of caring employees who want to improve their work situation and the products or services they generate. To make the art of root cause analysis more accessible to a larger audience, this book starts from scratch and gradually builds toward the objective of educating the reader in the basic skills of root cause analysis.

The book discusses many different tools for root cause analysis and presents these tools using an easy-to-follow structure: a general description of the tool, its purpose and typical applications, the procedure for using it, an example of its use, a checklist to help you make sure it is properly applied, and sample forms and templates (that can also be found on the enclosed CD-ROM). The examples are generic business examples that everyone should be able to recognize. Because this is not meant to be an academic book, you will not find the usual bibliographical references scattered throughout. However, to allow the reader to probe more deeply into some subjects, books treating different aspects of root cause analysis in more detail have been listed in the Additional Resources appendix at the end of the book. In this section, you'll also find a list of software that you can apply at different stages of root cause analysis.

The layout of the book has been designed to help speed your learning. Throughout, we have split the pages into two halves; the top half presents key concepts using brief language—almost keywords—and the bottom half shows examples to help explain the concepts. A navigation aid in the margin of each page simplifies navigating the book and searching for specific topics when the book is used as a root cause analysis dictionary.

The book is suited for employees and managers at any organizational level in any type of industry, including service, manufacturing, and public sector.

Our thanks to all the people who have inspired the writing of this book, including colleagues, classroom participants in our training courses, and companies with which we have worked. And our sincere thanks to all the great people at ASQ Quality Press who have performed excellently at every stage of the process.

Bjørn Andersen
Tom Fagerhaug
Trondheim, March 1, 2006

Chapter 1

Practical Problem Solving

Problem Solving

Root Cause
Analysis

Problem
Understanding

Problem Cause
Brainstorming

Problem Cause
Data Collection

Problem Cause
Data Analysis

Root Cause
Identification

Root Cause
Elimination

Solution
Implementation

Tool Selection

Example Cases

This chapter sets the pattern for the ensuing presentation of problem solving and root cause analysis. In it, we first define a problem, then give specific examples that illustrate the nature and types of problems that are discussed in this text. We discuss the different levels of causes for problems and introduce a general approach to practical problem solving.

Problem Solving

Root Cause Analysis

Problem Understanding

Problem Cause Brainstorming

Problem Cause Data Collection

Problem Cause Data Analysis

Root Cause Identification

Root Cause Elimination

Solution Implementation

Tool Selection

Example Cases

DEFINITION OF A PROBLEM

Problem: A question proposed for solution

Webster's Revised Unabridged Dictionary

A problem is a state of difficulty that needs to be resolved

Wordnet

These definitions suggest two characteristics of a problem that are important in our context:

- Having a problem is by nature a state of affairs plagued with some difficulty or undesired status.

- A problem represents a challenge that encourages solving to establish more desirable circumstances.

Types of Problems

From the two definitions of problem given above, it is evident that a problem can occur in any sphere of a person's life and take any form and shape. There may be practical problems in your private life, personal problems in your work situation, organizational problems within your department, and so on. This book deals with the general topic of root cause analysis and problem solving and, as such, is not limited to attacks on certain types of problems. Rather, the approaches described here can be applied to almost any kind of problem.

But the examples and cases used throughout the book deal exclusively with problems that occur within organizations. Our purpose in writing this book is a desire to help organizations solve problems that hinder their performance.

We are, however, convinced that the tools can also be applied by the parent who wants to spend more time with family or in solving personal problems. Therefore, if you wish to use the book to solve other types of problems, simply follow the instructions and adapt the lessons from the business-focused examples to your situation.

HOW TO SOLVE A PROBLEM

Beneath every problem lies a cause for that problem. Therefore, when trying to solve a problem, consider this approach:

1. Identify the cause (or causes) of the problem.

2. Find ways to eliminate these causes and prevent them from recurring.

This two-step approach may appear deceptively simple. But it is easy to underestimate the effort it sometimes takes to find the real causes of a problem. Once you've established the real causes, however, eliminating them is often a much easier task. Hence, identifying a problem's cause is paramount.

Problem Examples

A sawmill periodically suffered severe problems of accuracy when cutting lumber to different dimensions. "Experts" launched varying theories as to the causes for this, but the problems persisted. After thoroughly assessing the situation, the parties assigned to pinpoint the reasons for the deviations found the cause to be highly varying air temperature and humidity due to a poorly functioning air conditioning unit.

A car dealership had reorganized its operations to allow each employee to specialize in certain areas—sales, after-sales service, financing, and so on. One of the salespeople occasionally lost a sale because the credit evaluation undertaken by the finance department took too long, and the customer took their business elsewhere. It turned out that the person responsible for the credit checks deliberately stalled the process because he had felt overlooked when the specialized salespeople were selected.

Dimensional variation among lamp holders from certain suppliers caused a lot of rework for a lamp manufacturer. Adjustments that needed to be made to the lamp holders to ensure proper installation were estimated to cost more than $200,000 annually. Meanwhile, the procurement manager was pleased with himself because he had managed to reduce purchasing costs by about $50,000 the previous year by soliciting offers from many suppliers and buying from the one who offered the lowest price!

Problem Solving
Root Cause Analysis
Problem Understanding
Problem Cause Brainstorming
Problem Cause Data Collection
Problem Cause Data Analysis
Root Cause Identification
Root Cause Elimination
Solution Implementation
Tool Selection
Example Cases

Problem Solving

Root Cause Analysis

Problem Understanding

Problem Cause Brainstorming

Problem Cause Data Collection

Problem Cause Data Analysis

Root Cause Identification

Root Cause Elimination

Solution Implementation

Tool Selection

Example Cases

DIFFERENT LEVELS OF CAUSES

A problem is often the result of multiple causes at different levels. This means that some causes affect other causes that, in turn, create the visible problem. Causes can be classified as one of the following:

- *Symptoms.* These are not regarded as actual causes, but rather as signs of existing problems.

- *First-level causes.* Causes that directly lead to a problem.

- *Higher-level causes.* Causes that lead to the first-level causes. While they do not directly cause the problem, higher-level causes form links in the chain of cause-and-effect relationships that ultimately create the problem.

Some problems often have compound causes, where different factors combine to cause the problem. Examples of the levels of causes follow.

Examples of the Different Levels of Causes

Consider a paper producer that is having problems complying with the environmental regulations that apply to the industry. The industry's regulatory body has become aware of this situation and is constantly monitoring—and occasionally fining—the company for any breaches.

This problem could be defined as "unacceptable discharges of pollutants to water and air." In terms of the different levels of causes presented above, this problem is a result of the following causes:

- The symptoms are the fines issued by the regulatory body. Because the paper producer does not have an operating system for measuring the discharges, these fines represent the only way in which the company can detect occurrences of the problem. The fines can therefore be used as a "symptometer" that can be monitored to determine whether the problem has been eliminated or still recurs (much like a thermometer is used to monitor the presence of a fever, which indicates an inflammation).

- The first-level cause for the unacceptable discharges was that the company was slow to identify regulatory changes that affected its operations.

- More importantly, a chain of higher-level causes ultimately cost the company large sums in fines. These higher-level causes included the lack of an environmental management system, operating in a purely reactive mode, and the absence of an environment management strategy.

FIND THE ROOT CAUSE!

The highest-level cause of a problem is called the root cause:

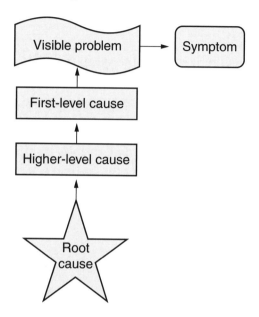

The root cause is "the evil at the bottom" that sets in motion the entire cause-and-effect chain causing the problem(s).

Two Examples of Root Causes

In the example of the paper producer, the highest-level cause, and thus the root cause, for unacceptable discharges was that the company had no environmental impact strategy. Such a strategy probably would have made the company more proactive regarding this issue: it might have paid more attention to new regulations and avoided illegal discharges.

When a hair dressing salon had to pay damages to customers because their hair was dyed the wrong color, the root cause was not that the hairdressers were poorly trained. Neither was it because, as some employees claimed, so little time was set aside for each customer that sloppiness resulted. The true root cause finally was discovered: the person who helped clean the salon returned opened bottles of dye to the wrong shelves. Why? Because she was color-blind and could not read the bottles.

You might find some of these root causes a little far-fetched. If so, take note of them even more. Problems such as those discussed here, which involve a number of different people and technical systems, are a cornucopia of different causes linked together in highly complex interrelationships. Consider the problems you face most often in your own organization—there could be equally unusual root causes at the heart of those problems! Again, the key issue is finding the root cause, be it extraordinary or commonplace.

Problem Solving

Root Cause Analysis

Problem Understanding

Problem Cause Brainstorming

Problem Cause Data Collection

Problem Cause Data Analysis

Root Cause Identification

Root Cause Elimination

Solution Implementation

Tool Selection

Example Cases

Problem Solving

Root Cause Analysis

Problem Understanding

Problem Cause Brainstorming

Problem Cause Data Collection

Problem Cause Data Analysis

Root Cause Identification

Root Cause Elimination

Solution Implementation

Tool Selection

Example Cases

ELIMINATE THE ROOT CAUSE!!

The discussion so far leads to the key recommendation of eliminating the true root cause(s). Other approaches might provide some temporary relief but will never produce a lasting solution:

- If you attack and remove only the symptoms, the situation can become worse. The problem will still be there, but there will no longer be an easily recognized symptom that can be monitored.

- Eliminating first- or higher-level causes may temporarily alleviate the problem, but the root cause will eventually find another way to manifest itself in the form of another problem.

When you have removed the root cause, monitor the symptoms to help ensure that the problem will not recur.

Root Cause Analysis and Problem Solving

So far, we have discussed the concept of a problem and the causes for problems. When we follow the chain of cause and effect behind a problem to its end, we discover the root cause. This can very well be the cause of many different problems, and it is most important to find and eliminate it.

The process of problem solving involves a number of steps, as illustrated on the following page. Important steps on the road to a solved problem are problem understanding, problem cause brainstorming, problem cause data collection, problem cause data analysis, root cause identification, root cause elimination, and solution implementation. Each of these steps poses different challenges and every one can be tricky at times. However, we maintain that finding the root cause is the crux of solving a problem. Without the root cause, there can be no lasting solution.

While we will present one possible approach to practical problem solving, the emphasis of this book is on root cause analysis. For more comprehensive coverage of different problem solving approaches, see the Additional Resources appendix at the end of the book.

A PROBLEM-SOLVING PROCESS

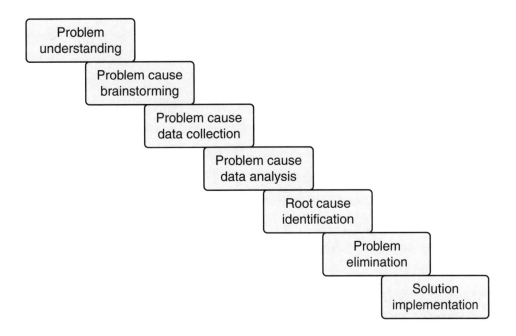

Problem understanding

Problem cause brainstorming

Problem cause data collection

Problem cause data analysis

Root cause identification

Problem elimination

Solution implementation

There Are Many Different Problem-Solving Approaches

The process for problem solving shown above is just one of many such models. Some emphasize the importance of testing and evaluating solutions before making them permanent, others focus on involving those who know the problem best in solving it, while some point out the importance of seeing the problem solving as part of a larger improvement effort. Another well-known approach is the Deming wheel, or the plan–do–check–act cycle:

The Deming wheel describes a systematic and continuous problem-solving approach. In the four respective phases, the problem is analyzed, rectifying measures are undertaken, the effects of these are evaluated, and the process is modified to encompass the activities that were confirmed to give results.

Problem Solving

Root Cause Analysis

Problem Understanding

Problem Cause Brainstorming

Problem Cause Data Collection

Problem Cause Data Analysis

Root Cause Identification

Root Cause Elimination

Solution Implementation

Tool Selection

Example Cases

THE STEPS IN PROBLEM SOLVING

The detailed steps in the problem-solving process are as follows:

- First, recognize that there is a problem. If you perceive the situation as normal, it will never improve.

- Then, call the problem by its real name; everyone affected by it must agree about this definition.

- Next, work to thoroughly understand the nature of the problem, as this forms the basis for ultimately solving it.

- Find the root cause.

- Only now are you able to attack—and ultimately eliminate—the root cause and thus prevent the problem from recurring.

- Lastly, monitor the symptoms signaling the presence of the problem to ensure success.

Some Problems Are Just Not Worth It

As you can see by the number of steps in a systematic approach to problem solving, the process can take some time and resources to accomplish the goal. Problems of minor importance, or of such a nature that they will likely go away by themselves given time, should not be the subject of such a comprehensive effort. It is simply not worth it, as the gains from removing the problem may be less than the costs of completing the process to remove it.

Likewise, it is unproductive to apply a complicated problem-solving process to commonplace problems we already know how to solve.

However, when you perceive the problem as important and don't know its nature or causes, attack it systematically to ensure that you find the root cause and ultimately eliminate the problem for good. In such cases, the problem-solving process makes sense and root cause analysis as presented in the remaining chapters will be important.

PROACTIVE PROBLEM PREVENTION COULD RENDER ROOT CAUSE ANALYSIS SUPERFLUOUS

While this book is dedicated to solving problems through eliminating their root causes, we should point out that this is an after-the-fact reactive response. At this stage, the problem has already materialized and may have done considerable damage.

Being ahead of such negative developments and proactively preventing problems from occurring in the first place is more effective than solving them after they appear. Effective problem prevention rests on:

- Thinking forward and beyond the immediate.

- Some degree of pessimism in the organization.

FMEA/FMECA Are Tools for Thinking Ahead

The focus of this book being on problem solving, we will not devote much space to problem prevention. If you are interested in pursuing the topic further, you should note that the various permutations of failure mode analysis (FMA) are useful tools in forcing the organization to think forward about problems that could occur. From basic FMA, several variants have evolved during the last couple of decades, including:

- *FMEA.* Failure mode and effects analysis, a tool that enables the identification and prevention of process or product errors before they occur. It is a systematic way to examine a process prospectively for possible ways in which failure can occur, and then to redesign the processes so that the new model eliminates the possibility of failure.

- *FMECA.* Failure modes, effects, and criticality analysis adds criticality assessments to the FMEA.

Both tools can contribute to improved designs for products and processes, resulting in higher reliability, better quality, increased safety, and reduced costs. These tools can also be used to establish maintenance plans for repairable systems and contribute to control plans and other quality assurance procedures. They provide a knowledge base of failure mode and corrective action information that can be used as a resource in future troubleshooting efforts. In addition, an FMEA or FMECA is often required to comply with safety and quality requirements, such as ISO 9001, QS 9000, ISO/TS 16949, Six Sigma, FDA Good Manufacturing Practices (GMPs), Process Safety Management (PSM) Act, and so on.

Follow up by prevention thinking!

Problem Solving

Root Cause Analysis

Problem Understanding

Problem Cause Brainstorming

Problem Cause Data Collection

Problem Cause Data Analysis

Root Cause Identification

Root Cause Elimination

Solution Implementation

Tool Selection

Example Cases

Chapter 2

Root Cause Analysis

Problem Solving

Root Cause Analysis

Problem Understanding

Problem Cause Brainstorming

Problem Cause Data Collection

Problem Cause Data Analysis

Root Cause Identification

Root Cause Elimination

Solution Implementation

Tool Selection

Example Cases

S o far, we have discussed problem solving in general and the importance of root cause analysis in practical problem solving. In this chapter, we define the nature of root cause analysis, how it is performed, and the different detailed approaches, techniques, and tools that make up the concept. This chapter presents the *contents* of the toolbox of root cause analysis; chapters 3 through 9 describe these tools in more detail.

Problem Solving
Root Cause Analysis
Problem Understanding
Problem Cause Brainstorming
Problem Cause Data Collection
Problem Cause Data Analysis
Root Cause Identification
Root Cause Elimination
Solution Implementation
Tool Selection
Example Cases

A DEFINITION OF ROOT CAUSE ANALYSIS

As far as we can determine, there is no generally accepted definition of what root cause analysis is. Therefore, we offer the following as a possible definition, one that at least communicates what is meant by the concept:

Root cause analysis is a structured investigation that aims to identify the true cause of a problem and the actions necessary to eliminate it.

While this sounds fairly straightforward, you will soon see that root cause analysis is not conducted using a single tool or strategy, but rather a number of tools, often used in combination.

Root Cause Analysis in a Larger Context

Taking a scholarly perspective, it is interesting to study which fields have led to the development of different concepts and ideas. The roots of root cause analysis, for example, can be traced to the broader field of total quality management, or TQM. TQM has developed in different directions more or less simultaneously. One of these directions is the development of a number of problem analysis, problem solving, and improvement tools. Today, TQM possesses a large toolbox of such techniques; root cause analysis is an integral part of this toolbox.

As indicated previously, root cause analysis is part of a more general problem-solving process. Further, problem solving is an integral part of continuous improvement. Thus, root cause analysis is one of the core building blocks in an organization's continuous improvement efforts. There are many books dealing with continuous improvement, so we won't cover this topic here. However, we feel it is important to keep in mind that root cause analysis in itself will not produce any results. It must be made part of a larger problem-solving effort, part of a conscious attitude that embraces a relentless pursuit of improvement at every level and in every department or business process of the organization.

WHAT IS ROOT CAUSE ANALYSIS?

Root cause analysis is a collective term used to describe a wide range of approaches, tools, and techniques used to uncover causes of problems.

Some of the approaches are geared more toward identifying the true root causes than others; some are more general problem-solving techniques, while others simply offer support for the core activity of root cause analysis. Some tools are characterized by a structured approach, while others are more creative (and haphazard) in nature.

The point is not to learn and apply all these tools, but rather to become acquainted with the root cause analysis toolbox and apply the appropriate technique or tool to address a specific problem.

Problem Solving
Root Cause Analysis
Problem Understanding
Problem Cause Brainstorming
Problem Cause Data Collection
Problem Cause Data Analysis
Root Cause Identification
Root Cause Elimination
Solution Implementation
Tool Selection
Example Cases

Root Cause Analysis Is Not the Only Overarching Concept

If you are confused by the fact that root cause analysis is not a streamlined process of a fixed number of steps, there might be some consolation in the fact that many of the tools and techniques of TQM provide the overarching concepts. Some of the more important of these are:

- Problem solving

- Business process reengineering or improvement

- Benchmarking

- Continuous improvement

All of these are often presented as if they were single tools, while in fact they cover a varying number of individual tools that are applied in a structured manner.

GROUPS OF ROOT CAUSE ANALYSIS TOOLS

We have grouped the different root cause analysis tools according to their purpose, and at which point they are typically used, for these reasons:

- There are so many tools that it is necessary to maintain clarity throughout the presentation of them.

- They naturally fall into categories of tools that serve slightly different purposes.

The groups of tools, according to their purpose, are:

- Problem understanding

- Problem cause brainstorming

- Problem cause data collection

- Problem cause data analysis

- Root cause identification

- Root cause elimination

- Solution implementation

But be aware that many of the tools can be used at other times and for other purposes as well.

Different Means to the Same End

These groups of tools contribute in their own way to the root cause analysis. Some are best applied sequentially; others can be applied at many different points in the analysis:

- *Problem understanding.* Methods that help get to the bottom of a problem. This phase focuses on understanding the nature of the problem, and is a first step before starting the analysis.

- *Problem cause brainstorming.* Generic tools that can be applied at different stages in the analysis. Brainstorming can help generate ideas about possible causes. Since the analysis normally is carried out in groups, methods that help you arrive at consensus solutions are also useful.

Continued

Continued

- *Problem cause data collection.* These generic tools and techniques are used to systematically and efficiently collect data related to a problem and its probable cause.

- *Problem cause data analysis.* Tools used for making the most of the data collected about the problem. When analyzing the same data from different angles, different conclusions might emerge. Some conclusions may not uncover the problem's causes, so it is important to have several data analyzing tools available.

- *Root cause identification.* The heart of root cause analysis. Root cause analysis is not one single approach, and neither is this group of tools. You can use these tools to more deeply analyze the problem's root cause(s).

- *Root cause elimination.* Devising solutions that will remove the root cause and thus eliminate the problem.

- *Solution implementation.* Techniques and advice to aid the change process of implementing the solution.

Problem Solving

Root Cause Analysis

Problem Understanding

Problem Cause Brainstorming

Problem Cause Data Collection

Problem Cause Data Analysis

Root Cause Identification

Root Cause Elimination

Solution Implementation

Tool Selection

Example Cases

Problem Solving

Root Cause Analysis

Problem Understanding

Problem Cause Brainstorming

Problem Cause Data Collection

Problem Cause Data Analysis

Root Cause Identification

Root Cause Elimination

Solution Implementation

Tool Selection

Example Cases

THE INDIVIDUAL ROOT CAUSE ANALYSIS TOOLS

Problem Understanding

- *Flowcharts.* Charts used to "paint a picture" of business processes.

- *Critical incident.* An elegant approach used to explore the most critical issues in a situation.

- *Spider chart.* A comparison chart used to benchmark problems.

- *Performance matrix.* Used to help determine the importance of problems or causes.

Problem Cause Brainstorming

- *Brainstorming.* A formal approach that can be applied throughout the root cause analysis when multiple ideas are required.

- *Brainwriting.* In effect, a written brainstorming session.

- *Is–is not matrix.* A matrix tool to help separate factors in a problem that are relevant from those that are not.

- *Nominal group technique.* A technique used to help a group prioritize different alternatives, for example, possible problem causes.

- *Paired comparisons.* A technique used to reach consensus by allowing participants to choose between pairs of two competing alternatives.

Problem Cause Data Collection

- *Sampling.* Used to surmise data on a large population by collecting only a small sample.

- *Surveys.* Used to collect data about opinions and attitudes from customers, employees, and so on.

- *Check sheet.* A useful approach that systematically collects data based on predefined sheets that are applied throughout the collection period.

Problem Cause Data Analysis

- *Histogram.* An easy-to-use visual diagram that helps identify patterns or anomalies.

- *Pareto chart.* Another visual tool used to illustrate which causes generate the most effects.

- *Scatter chart.* Used to illustrate relationships between two causes or other variables in the problem situation.

- *Problem concentration diagram.* A visual chart that maps the layout or structure of a site or system and is used to identify where problems occur.

- *Relations diagram.* A tool used to identify logical relationships between different ideas or issues in a complex or confusing situation.

- *Affinity diagram.* A chart that helps correlate seemingly unrelated ideas, causes, or other concepts so they might collectively be explored further.

Root Cause Identification

- *Cause-and-effect chart.* An easily applied tool used to analyze possible causes of a problem.

- *Matrix diagram.* A visual technique for spotting relationships between factors and analyzing causal relationships between them. The diagram can thus be used to determine which of different possible causes contribute the most to a problem.

- *Five whys.* An approach used to delve ever more deeply into causal relationships.

- *Fault tree analysis.* A tool for looking forward and anticipating what problems can occur in a system, product, or business process.

Root Cause Elimination

- *Six thinking hats.* A technique to force people to change their perspective and think according to different roles.

- *Theory of inventive problem solving (TRIZ).* A technique based on breaking down a problem into recognizable standard engineering problems with known solutions.

Problem Solving

Root Cause Analysis

Problem Understanding

Problem Cause Brainstorming

Problem Cause Data Collection

Problem Cause Data Analysis

Root Cause Identification

Root Cause Elimination

Solution Implementation

Tool Selection

Example Cases

Problem Solving
Root Cause Analysis
Problem Understanding
Problem Cause Brainstorming
Problem Cause Data Collection
Problem Cause Data Analysis
Root Cause Identification
Root Cause Elimination
Solution Implementation
Tool Selection
Example Cases

- *Systematic inventive thinking (SIT).* A tool building further on TRIZ, containing four principles for approaching a problem and its components.

Solution Implementation

- *Tree diagram.* Used for planning a project, for example an improvement implementation.

- *Force-field analysis.* Used to identify forces working for and against an improvement implementation.

Each of these tools and techniques is described in detail in chapters 3 through 9. We would like to point out that conducting a root cause analysis often involves applying several of these tools, either in sequence or in multiple iterations using the same tool. In the end, finding the true root cause can involve several rounds of "drilling down" into the problem and its levels of symptoms and causes.

CONDUCTING A ROOT CAUSE ANALYSIS

Root cause analysis is a highly versatile analysis approach. These are some useful hints for carrying out this analysis:

- Many of the individual root cause analysis tools can be used by a single person. Nevertheless, the outcome generally is better when they are applied by a group of people who work together to find the problem causes.

- Those ultimately responsible for removing the identified root cause(s) should be prominent members of the analysis team that sets out to uncover them.

- Treat the titles of the groups of tools as indicative of their primary purpose. During the analysis, apply tools and approaches with which the team is familiar and that seem to fit.

The Logistics of a Root Cause Analysis

As root cause analysis is a collection of many techniques, it is difficult to outline a more detailed procedure than the sequence represented by the chapters of this book. As an example, however, the following represents a typical design of a root cause analysis in an organization:

- A small team is formed to conduct the root cause analysis.

- Team members are selected from the business process/area of the organization that experiences the problem, supplemented by a line manager with decision authority to implement solutions, an internal customer from the process with problems, and possibly a quality improvement expert in the case where the other team members have little experience with this kind of work.

- The analysis lasts about two months, relatively evenly distributed between defining and understanding the problem, brainstorming its possible causes, analyzing causes and effects, and devising a solution to the problem.

- During this period, the team meets at least weekly, some times two or three times a week. The meetings are always kept short, at maximum two hours, and since they are meant to be creative in nature, the agenda is quite loose.

Continued

Problem Solving

Root Cause Analysis

Problem Understanding

Problem Cause Brainstorming

Problem Cause Data Collection

Problem Cause Data Analysis

Root Cause Identification

Root Cause Elimination

Solution Implementation

Tool Selection

Example Cases

Continued

Problem Solving

Root Cause Analysis

Problem Understanding

Problem Cause Brainstorming

Problem Cause Data Collection

Problem Cause Data Analysis

Root Cause Identification

Root Cause Elimination

Solution Implementation

Tool Selection

Example Cases

- One person in the team is assigned the role of making sure the analysis progresses, or tasks are assigned to various members of the team.

- Once the solution has been designed and the decision to implement has been taken, it can take anywhere from a day to several months before the change is complete, depending on what is involved in the implementation process.

Chapter 3

Tools for Problem Understanding

Problem Solving

Root Cause
Analysis

**Problem
Understanding**

Problem Cause
Brainstorming

Problem Cause
Data Collection

Problem Cause
Data Analysis

Root Cause
Identification

Root Cause
Elimination

Solution
Implementation

Tool Selection

Example Cases

So far, we have laid the groundwork for the details of the root cause analysis. In this and the following chapters, we present each of the different tools and techniques briefly mentioned in Chapter 2. We have adhered to a common structure for all tools: a general description of the tool, its purpose and typical applications, the procedure for its use, an example of its use, a checklist to help ensure that it is applied properly, and sample forms and templates that can be photocopied from the book or copied to your computer from the CD-ROM. This chapter deals specifically with how to gain a solid understanding of the problem that needs to be solved.

Problem Solving

Root Cause Analysis

Problem Understanding

Problem Cause Brainstorming

Problem Cause Data Collection

Problem Cause Data Analysis

Root Cause Identification

Root Cause Elimination

Solution Implementation

Tool Selection

Example Cases

PROBLEM UNDERSTANDING

To ensure that your root cause analysis efforts are directed at the right problem, you must first understand the problem. The tools to help you do this are:

- Flowchart

- Critical incident

- Spider chart

- Performance matrix

The Importance of Problem Understanding

A newspaper printing company, fully owned by the newspaper it printed, also took on printing jobs for external customers. There were often scheduling problems when planning the printing of the newspaper (including second editions in cases of breaking news, advertising sections for the following day, and so on) and combining these with the external jobs. As a result, overtime was paid to complete all jobs. To attack this problem, the printing company invested in a sophisticated computerized production planning software package. And nothing improved!

When looking more thoroughly into the problem, the company discovered that it was paying for having capacity reserved for its production. (These payments covered the hourly costs for the presses and the wages for the operators.) When the newspaper used the reserved capacity, it also paid for the paper, ink, and so on. However, when the same capacity, which often remained unused by the newspaper, was sold to external customers, they also paid for the machine usage, wages, and materials. Therefore the company was receiving payment from two sources for the same capacity.

As tempting as this questionable arrangement was, the printing company often double-sold this reserved capacity, gambling that the newspaper would not use it. The deal between the printing company and the newspaper—and not the production planning—was the problem.

THE PURPOSE AND APPLICATIONS OF FLOWCHARTS

Many of the problems that occur in organizations are connected to the business or work processes that are carried out there. Thus, as a first step in root cause analysis, making a flowchart of business processes is appropriate.

The main purpose of a flowchart is to portray the flow of activities in a process. As a first step in root cause analysis, flowcharts can be used to:

- Map a process to illustrate where problems occur and which problems should be solved.

- Provide a basis for an ensuing root cause analysis by providing a detailed understanding of the process(es) that contain or influence the problem.

Different Types of Flowcharts

Flowcharts come in many shapes and sizes. Some have been designed with special purposes in mind; others are simply variations that allow more or less information to be included within them. While this book does not pretend to cover flowcharting in detail, it is pertinent to mention some of the more useful types of flowcharts in terms of root cause analysis. These are:

- *Regular flowchart*, which simply depicts a sequence of activities or tasks and contains no other information.

- *Cross-functional flowchart*, which additionally indicates which person or department is responsible for each of the activities or tasks. This flowchart can also contain information on the duration of the activities, how much they cost, and so on.

- *Flowcharts on several levels*, which enable adding more detail to the charts. A simple flowchart usually forms the top-level chart, which gives a clear overview of the process. To provide information about certain steps in the process without clouding the top-level picture, each step is detailed in a new chart on a level below. For very complex processes, there can be many such levels of charts.

Of these, we cover only the regular flowchart in this chapter, mainly because the other types build on this.

Problem Solving

Root Cause Analysis

Problem Understanding

Problem Cause Brainstorming

Problem Cause Data Collection

Problem Cause Data Analysis

Root Cause Identification

Root Cause Elimination

Solution Implementation

Tool Selection

Example Cases

Problem Solving

Root Cause
Analysis

**Problem
Understanding**

Problem Cause
Brainstorming

Problem Cause
Data Collection

Problem Cause
Data Analysis

Root Cause
Identification

Root Cause
Elimination

Solution
Implementation

Tool Selection

Example Cases

THE STEPS IN USING FLOWCHARTS

1. Gather those working in the process to be documented in a meeting room with whiteboard facilities and plenty of adhesive notes in different colors.

2. Define the customers (internal or external) of the process, the output they receive, the input needed for the process, and the suppliers of that input.

3. Identify the main activities or tasks undertaken during the process to convert input to output, preferably starting with the end product/service and working backward.

4. Use adhesive notes in different colors to represent activities, products, documents, and other elements of the process.

5. Map the process by moving the notes around until they reflect the most realistic picture of the current process.

6. If there is a need to store the flowchart electronically, enter the chart into a computer.

An Example of the Use of a Flowchart

A manufacturer of machines for paper mills had refined a design philosophy whereby almost 100 percent of the parts needed were purchased; the core competency of the company, therefore, was in innovative designs, integration management, and assembly.

Many of these component parts were complex and could rarely be purchased on the spot. Rather, long-term agreements were often necessary and, in many cases, provided better deals. Other parts, like nuts and bolts, standard electric parts, and so forth, could be bought from almost any supplier able to deliver. Over several months, many purchasing agents had left the company and were replaced by new ones. This led to many problems, such as higher prices for various parts, poor delivery performance of incoming parts, lower quality, and so forth.

Both to train new purchasers and to have a starting point for a closer analysis of these problems, a flowchart of the purchasing process was made. This process could be divided into five distinct phases, so the flowchart was made up of two levels. One covered the overall process while the next level contained more detailed maps of each of the five process segments. The overall chart and one of the detailed charts are shown on the next page.

FLOWCHARTS EXAMPLE—PAPER MILL

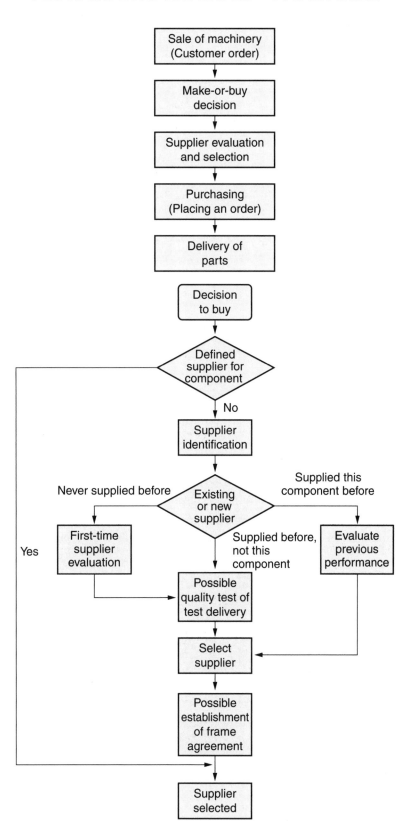

Problem Solving

Root Cause Analysis

Problem Understanding

Problem Cause Brainstorming

Problem Cause Data Collection

Problem Cause Data Analysis

Root Cause Identification

Root Cause Elimination

Solution Implementation

Tool Selection

Example Cases

Problem Solving

Root Cause
Analysis

**Problem
Understanding**

Problem Cause
Brainstorming

Problem Cause
Data Collection

Problem Cause
Data Analysis

Root Cause
Identification

Root Cause
Elimination

Solution
Implementation

Tool Selection

Example Cases

CHECKLIST FOR FLOWCHARTS

❑ Include all (or at least a majority) of those working
in the process to be flowcharted in the activity. It is
important to have all departments represented in the
process included in the documentation task, both to
ensure access to all necessary information and to
create ownership of the end result. Furthermore, a
supplier or customer, internal or external, may offer
additional insight into the process.

❑ Perform an initial identification of the boundaries of
the process, focusing on customers, output, input, and
suppliers.

❑ Identify the main activities of the process that are
carried out to convert the inputs to outputs.

❑ Represent all activities in the process—inputs, outputs,
and so on—using adhesive notes in different colors.

❑ Move the adhesive notes around until they accurately
depict the process being reviewed.

❑ If desired, add information to make the flowchart a
cross-functional chart or a chart with several levels.

❑ When participants agree on the look of the flowchart,
store the design on a computer (if there is a need
for this).

❑ Use this flowchart as a picture of the process when
applying other tools.

THE PURPOSE AND APPLICATIONS OF CRITICAL INCIDENT

When beginning to solve a problem, many work simply from a gut feeling about what the problem really is. Finding the root cause of the problem, and ultimately its solution, would be easier if the true crux of the problem was acknowledged.

The main purpose of the critical incident method is to understand what the most troublesome symptoms in a problematic situation really are. Critical incident analysis helps you:

- Understand which aspects of the problem need to be solved.

- Realize the nature of the problem and its consequences.

Openness Is a Prerequisite

Most of the tools in root cause analysis have two things in common:

- They are best applied by a team of people working together to find the problem's causes and solve them.

- To work properly, they require an atmosphere of trust, openness, and honesty that encourages people to divulge important information without fearing consequences.

If this climate is not provided, chances are that the root cause analysis will fail to bring to the surface the true nature of the problem or its causes. Creating this climate is everyone's responsibility, but management clearly holds a special position, as they possess the most instruments for achieving this. This applies to all of the tools presented in this book, but it is pertinent especially with the critical incident method, as it may bring to light potentially embarrassing situations.

Problem Solving

Root Cause Analysis

Problem Understanding

Problem Cause Brainstorming

Problem Cause Data Collection

Problem Cause Data Analysis

Root Cause Identification

Root Cause Elimination

Solution Implementation

Tool Selection

Example Cases

<table>
<tr><td>Problem Solving</td></tr>
<tr><td>Root Cause Analysis</td></tr>
<tr><td>**Problem Understanding**</td></tr>
<tr><td>Problem Cause Brainstorming</td></tr>
<tr><td>Problem Cause Data Collection</td></tr>
<tr><td>Problem Cause Data Analysis</td></tr>
<tr><td>Root Cause Identification</td></tr>
<tr><td>Root Cause Elimination</td></tr>
<tr><td>Solution Implementation</td></tr>
<tr><td>Tool Selection</td></tr>
<tr><td>Example Cases</td></tr>
</table>

THE STEPS IN USING CRITICAL INCIDENT

1. Decide on the participants to be included, attempting to cover all departments or functional areas involved in the problem situation.

2. Ask each participant to answer in writing questions like: Which incident last week was most difficult to handle? Which episode created the biggest problems in terms of maintaining customer satisfaction? Which incident cost the most in terms of extra resources or direct expenditures?

3. Collect, sort, and analyze answers based on the frequency of different incidents.

4. Graphically present the sorted list to show the criticality of each incident.

5. Use the most critical incidents as starting points for the search for problem causes.

An Example of the Use of Critical Incident

Having grown considerably during the last two years, what once was a very small two-man management consulting firm had now become a successful outfit employing about 75 consultants. Since most of the problems the clients wanted solved were of a multidisciplinary nature, the company made it standard procedure to visit potential clients in pairs or even in threes.

Although no specific debate was ever started, there were some rumblings in the hallways and rumors going around that this sales technique was not very effective. Since no one was able to tell exactly what was wrong with it or what should be done differently, nothing happened to change it.

However, after a particularly frustrating visit to an important client, two of the consultants initiated a critical incident session to get to the bottom of the frustration. The consultants had themselves used the critical incident approach with clients many times and knew it well, but had never tried it internally. Nevertheless, it all went smoothly and generated some valuable insights.

The critical incidents identified by one of the consultants are shown on the top of the next page, while a summary of the entire investigation is shown below it. It turned out that the real problem with the sales approach was that the consultants, who make a living out of their credibility, often ended up looking silly, in disagreement, or generally feeling embarrassed in front of clients.

CRITICAL INCIDENT EXAMPLE—
SALES VISITS

Sales Visits to Clients:
Critical Incidents

- Suggesting a different solution than Thomas at SysCom
- Quoting an hourly rate in the meeting instead of in a written offer
- Being late for the meeting with ADA
- Showing up without having had the time to prepare properly

Type of incident	Frequency
Embarrassment by disagreeing with colleague	112
Being unprepared, thus giving a bad impression	39
Revealing too much information about prices or approaches	21
Losing a client to a competitor	14
Being late for meetings when the partner is already there	8
Not being able to suggest solutions to the client's problem	8
Feeling an obvious lack of chemistry with the client	5
Getting into an argument with the client	3
Spilling coffee on the client	1

Problem Solving

Root Cause Analysis

Problem Understanding

Problem Cause Brainstorming

Problem Cause Data Collection

Problem Cause Data Analysis

Root Cause Identification

Root Cause Elimination

Solution Implementation

Tool Selection

Example Cases

Problem Solving

Root Cause
Analysis

**Problem
Understanding**

Problem Cause
Brainstorming

Problem Cause
Data Collection

Problem Cause
Data Analysis

Root Cause
Identification

Root Cause
Elimination

Solution
Implementation

Tool Selection

Example Cases

CHECKLIST FOR CRITICAL INCIDENT

❏ Assemble a group of participants for the critical incident session. The participants should represent all departments or functional areas of the company that are involved in or related to the problem situation.

❏ Ask each participant individually to write down answers to one or more predefined questions. The questions should cover issues related to the problem situation and which aspects cause the most problems, cost the most, generate the most negative publicity, and so on.

❏ Collect the answers and sort them according to frequency of mention; analyze them for any patterns.

❏ Present the sorted list of incidents graphically, if necessary.

❏ Use the most critical incidents as starting points for an ensuing search for causes to the problem.

THE PURPOSE AND APPLICATIONS OF SPIDER CHARTS

Flowcharts and critical incident aid in understanding the problem from an internal point of view. When seeking an external comparison, a spider chart can be a helpful tool. The main purpose of the spider chart is to give a graphical impression of how the performance of business processes (or problem areas) compares with other organizations. In root cause analysis, the main applications of a spider chart are to:

- Determine which problem is most critical.

- Compare the seriousness of problems and causes.

A Spider Chart Is a Way of Benchmarking

Benchmarking means comparing performance levels or practices with someone else, preferably someone with superior performance. Such comparison serves many purposes, including:

- Motivating improvement by demonstrating that someone has solved a problem or reached higher levels of performance, thus showing that it is possible.

- Providing input as to what objectives should be set for the improvements stemming from problem solving and other improvement efforts, based on the achievement of others.

- Learning how to do better by obtaining ideas and inspiration from those who are better than yourself.

Furthermore, benchmarking against others can help you identify which areas of your operations need improvement and which are doing well already. This type of benchmarking can be facilitated by the use of a spider chart, as it allows comparing the performance levels of different processes or areas against others. Based on the results, the organization will get some direction as to where improvements are most needed.

Problem Solving

Root Cause Analysis

Problem Understanding

Problem Cause Brainstorming

Problem Cause Data Collection

Problem Cause Data Analysis

Root Cause Identification

Root Cause Elimination

Solution Implementation

Tool Selection

Example Cases

THE STEPS IN USING SPIDER CHARTS

1. Collect the information needed to construct the spider chart—typically data from market analyses, surveys, competitor analyses, and so on.

2. Assign one variable to each spoke in the chart.

3. Divide each spoke into logical segments by using a separate unit of measurement for each variable. The farther from the center of the chart, the higher the performance.

4. Plot the performance data for each variable along the correct spokes, using different colors or symbols to separate the data points from different organizations.

5. Draw lines between the data points for each organization to generate performance profiles.

6. Identify the variables that show the largest gaps between your organization and the benchmarks.

An Example of the Use of a Spider Chart

An average-sized social welfare office in a large city had a number of problems to cope with at any given time. One of the most serious of these was related to the security of the employees. The office had seen verbal abuse, physical assaults on case workers, unrest among waiting clients, and one instance of a serious stabbing of an employee.

The issue of employee safety had a number of different facets. Before trying to identify and remove the causes to any specific threats, it was necessary to rate which types of threats were most serious. Because matters of personal safety tend to make people think less rationally than when they face more neutral problems, it was unlikely that simply discussing the question among the employees would lead to a thorough understanding of the situation.

Because the state government regularly collected data on such problems from all offices in the state, comparing this office against others and state averages would be easy. Thus, office employees decided to construct a spider chart based on this data. The factors assigned to the spokes in the chart are listed on the top of the next page, while the chart is displayed below the list. From this chart, employees formed a clear picture as to which factors were especially severe when compared with the rest of the offices—namely, verbal abuse and threats and serious property damage.

SPIDER CHART EXAMPLE—SOCIAL WELFARE OFFICE

Chart Categories (Frequency of Occurrence)

I.   Verbal abuse from clients

II.   Verbal threats by clients

III.   Minor physical abuse from clients

IV.   More serious physical abuse from clients

V.   Serious injuries inflicted by clients

VI.   Murders committed by clients

VII.   Minor property damage by clients

VIII.   Serious property damage by clients

Problem Solving
Root Cause Analysis
Problem Understanding
Problem Cause Brainstorming
Problem Cause Data Collection
Problem Cause Data Analysis
Root Cause Identification
Root Cause Elimination
Solution Implementation
Tool Selection
Example Cases

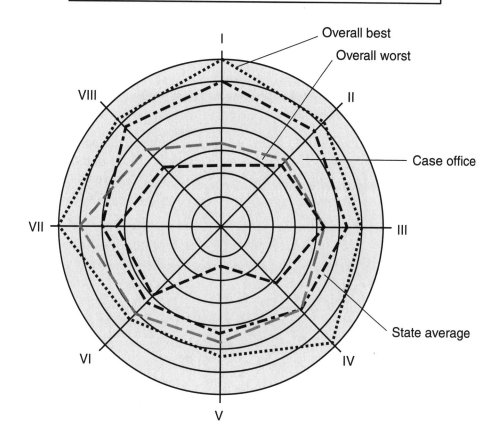

Problem Solving

Root Cause
Analysis

**Problem
Understanding**

Problem Cause
Brainstorming

Problem Cause
Data Collection

Problem Cause
Data Analysis

Root Cause
Identification

Root Cause
Elimination

Solution
Implementation

Tool Selection

Example Cases

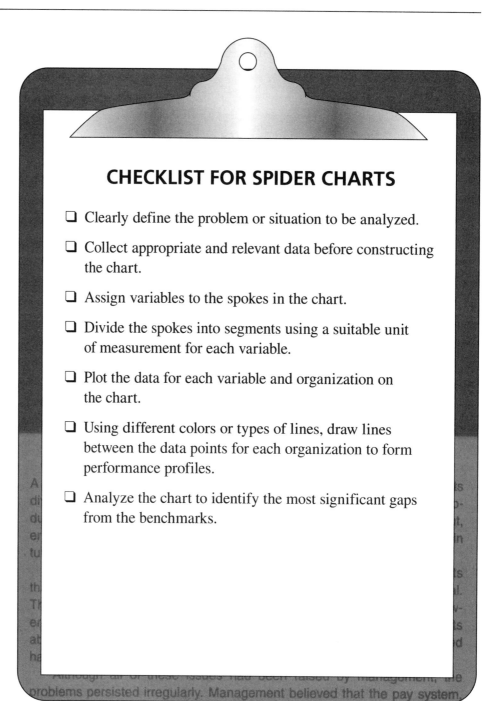

CHECKLIST FOR SPIDER CHARTS

❑ Clearly define the problem or situation to be analyzed.

❑ Collect appropriate and relevant data before constructing the chart.

❑ Assign variables to the spokes in the chart.

❑ Divide the spokes into segments using a suitable unit of measurement for each variable.

❑ Plot the data for each variable and organization on the chart.

❑ Using different colors or types of lines, draw lines between the data points for each organization to form performance profiles.

❑ Analyze the chart to identify the most significant gaps from the benchmarks.

SPIDER CHART TEMPLATE

Chart Categories

I.

II.

III.

IV.

V.

VI.

VII.

VIII.

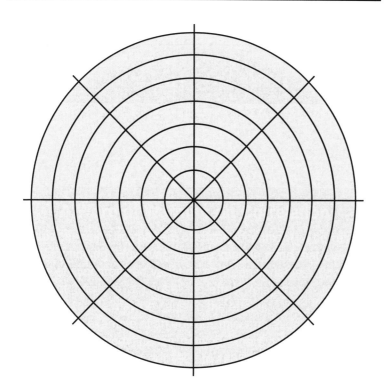

Problem Solving

Root Cause Analysis

Problem Understanding

Problem Cause Brainstorming

Problem Cause Data Collection

Problem Cause Data Analysis

Root Cause Identification

Root Cause Elimination

Solution Implementation

Tool Selection

Example Cases

Problem Solving

Root Cause Analysis

Problem Understanding

Problem Cause Brainstorming

Problem Cause Data Collection

Problem Cause Data Analysis

Root Cause Identification

Root Cause Elimination

Solution Implementation

Tool Selection

Example Cases

THE PURPOSE AND APPLICATIONS OF PERFORMANCE MATRICES

When comparing the different aspects of a spider chart, the focus is solely on the performance of the variables included in the chart. An equally relevant aspect to consider along with the current performance level, however, is the importance of each variable. The performance matrix is used to illustrate current performance and importance at the same time, helping to arrive at a sense of priority.

In root cause analysis, performance matrices can be used to illustrate problems or causes in terms of:

- Which aspect of the problem is most important to attack

- Which causes will give the most relief if removed

Four Quadrants of the Matrix

Factors being analyzed are placed in a matrix diagram. The area is divided into four sectors on the basis of current performance and importance of the factors.

The meaning of each quadrant is as follows:

- *Unimportant* (low importance, low performance). The performance level of this aspect of the problem is low, but its low importance renders it unnecessary to improve this particular issue.

- *Overkill* (low importance, high performance). The performance level of this aspect of the problem is high, but this is of less consequence because the issues in this quadrant are not especially important. Therefore, this is not a candidate for improvement.

- *Must be improved* (high importance, low performance). Factors that fall within this area are important, while the current performance level is low. This is an obvious area for starting improvements.

- *OK* (high importance, high performance). A golden rule is that areas where the performance is already good also should be improved. However, factors that—in addition to being important—are not being performed well today *(must be improved)*, should be improved first. If no factors fall within that quadrant, issues in the OK quadrant are the second choice for improvement.

THE STEPS IN USING PERFORMANCE MATRICES

1. Construct an empty chart by placing importance on the horizontal axis and current performance on the vertical axis and dividing both axes into nine segments of equal size.

2. Decide which problems, factors, or issues to analyze.

3. Place each factor in the chart according to its position along the two axes, using symbols to identify each factor.

4. Divide the chart into four quadrants approximately at the middle of each axis. If many factors are clustered in one area, place the division lines farther to one side.

5. Determine which factors fall within the quadrants.

An Example of the Use of a Performance Matrix

Because performance matrices are closely linked to spider charts, the example of the performance matrix is a follow-up to the previous example. From the spider chart, the social welfare office concluded that verbal abuse and threats and serious property damage were most prominent compared with other similar offices.

Because these conclusions focused on less serious dangers to the employees, a performance matrix analysis was used as a supplement. The same factors were plotted in a matrix according to assessments of their performance and importance. (The completed matrix is shown on the following page.) The division lines between the quadrants were moved somewhat off center because some clusters were evident.

From this matrix, office workers concluded that the issue of serious property damage (category VIII) was still important. However, due to the much higher importance assessments of the physical danger factors by the employees, compared with merely verbal abuse, these four issues (categories III thru VI) were more heavily weighted at the expense of verbal abuse and threats (categories I and II).

Problem Solving

Root Cause Analysis

Problem Understanding

Problem Cause Brainstorming

Problem Cause Data Collection

Problem Cause Data Analysis

Root Cause Identification

Root Cause Elimination

Solution Implementation

Tool Selection

Example Cases

Problem Solving

Root Cause Analysis

Problem Understanding

Problem Cause Brainstorming

Problem Cause Data Collection

Problem Cause Data Analysis

Root Cause Identification

Root Cause Elimination

Solution Implementation

Tool Selection

Example Cases

PERFORMANCE MATRIX EXAMPLE—SOCIAL WELFARE OFFICE

Chart Categories (Frequency of Occurrence)

I. Verbal abuse from clients

II. Verbal threats by clients

III. Minor physical abuse from clients

IV. More serious physical abuse from clients

V. Serious injuries inflicted by clients

VI. Murders committed by clients

VII. Minor property damage by clients

VIII. Serious property damage by clients

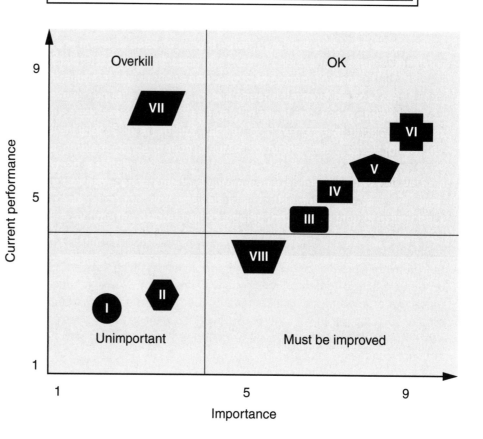

CHECKLIST FOR
PERFORMANCE MATRICES

❑ Construct a chart with importance on the horizontal axis and current performance on the vertical, with the axes divided into nine equal segments.

❑ Decide which factors will be analyzed.

❑ Plot all factors on the chart based on the assessments/ measurements of their importance and current performance.

❑ Use different symbols to identify each factor when plotting the factors on the chart.

❑ Divide the chart into quadrants. Draw division lines from the center of each axis, skewing as needed if clusters are evident.

❑ Identify the factors within each quadrant, using the *must be improved* factors as a starting point for further actions.

Problem Solving

Root Cause Analysis

Problem Understanding

Problem Cause Brainstorming

Problem Cause Data Collection

Problem Cause Data Analysis

Root Cause Identification

Root Cause Elimination

Solution Implementation

Tool Selection

Example Cases

Problem Solving

Root Cause
Analysis

**Problem
Understanding**

Problem Cause
Brainstorming

Problem Cause
Data Collection

Problem Cause
Data Analysis

Root Cause
Identification

Root Cause
Elimination

Solution
Implementation

Tool Selection

Example Cases

PERFORMANCE MATRIX TEMPLATE

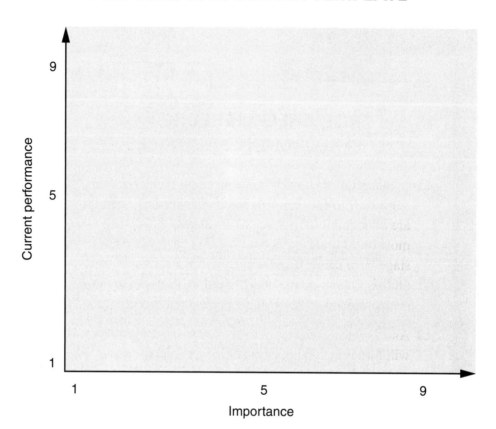

PROBLEM UNDERSTANDING CHECKLIST

❑ Although root cause analysis is not one clear process from start to finish, some distinct stages in the analysis are discernible. This checklist helps assess whether the most important elements of the problem understanding stage have been accomplished before moving on. Agree on the problem to be attacked before embarking on the root cause analysis.

❑ Assess the situation in which problem understanding will be undertaken to select a suitable approach. Typical considerations are pre-analysis problem understanding, how many people have been involved in debates about the problem thus far, and so on.

❑ Choose among the following tools and approaches: flowchart, critical incident, spider chart, and performance matrix.

❑ Achieve a common understanding of the problem, its seriousness, and its consequences, through use of the selected tools.

❑ Bring the problem understanding forward into the problem cause brainstorming stage.

Problem Solving

Root Cause Analysis

Problem Understanding

Problem Cause Brainstorming

Problem Cause Data Collection

Problem Cause Data Analysis

Root Cause Identification

Root Cause Elimination

Solution Implementation

Tool Selection

Example Cases

4

Tools for Problem Cause Brainstorming

Problem Solving

Root Cause Analysis

Problem Understanding

Problem Cause Brainstorming

Problem Cause Data Collection

Problem Cause Data Analysis

Root Cause Identification

Root Cause Elimination

Solution Implementation

Tool Selection

Example Cases

Chapter 4 presents idea-generating tools to help determine possible causes of a problem as well as tools the team can use to reach agreement in cases of disputes or differing views.

Problem Solving

Root Cause Analysis

Problem Understanding

Problem Cause Brainstorming

Problem Cause Data Collection

Problem Cause Data Analysis

Root Cause Identification

Root Cause Elimination

Solution Implementation

Tool Selection

Example Cases

PROBLEM CAUSE BRAINSTORMING

Often a suspicion exists as to what causes the problem you are trying to solve. But before you rush off to test your hypothesis, consider other candidates. This is what possible cause brainstorming is all about. Additionally, having an arsenal of tools for reaching agreement when the team disagrees is important.

The tools available in this stage are:

• Brainstorming

• Brainwriting

• Is–is not matrix

• Nominal group technique

• Paired comparisons

Avoid Running off in Different Directions

Five highly trained waiters on a cruise ship were given the task of finding out what caused long waiting lines during some meals and not during others. The team started capturing the characteristics of meals resulting in queues, such as time of the week, the menu, the program for the day, and so on.

When deciding how to proceed, either by trying to vary these conditions to measure the effects or by conducting interviews with some guests, the team ran into a deadlock: three opted for the former approach, two for the latter. They never managed to set aside their differences and the team disbanded.

THE PURPOSE AND APPLICATIONS OF BRAINSTORMING

The problems we face in our work life rarely have one easily identifiable cause. Finding their root cause requires creativity!

Brainstorming is a great way to generate as many good ideas as possible related to a given subject. Its purpose is to:

- Generate a list of problem areas that can be improved.

- Identify possible consequences stemming from the problem being analyzed.

- Generate a list of possible causes of the problem.

- Encourage thinking about ways to eliminate the causes.

Two Types of Brainstorming

In root cause analysis, brainstorming is not one single, well-defined activity. Actually, there are two different ways to brainstorm:

- *Structured brainstorming*, where each participant in turn launches one idea, is more structured and ensures equal participation, but is less spontaneous and to some extent limits the possibility for building on one another's ideas. This type of approach is called round-robin brainstorming.

- *Unstructured brainstorming*, where everyone can freely launch ideas, is very spontaneous, but is often more confusing and can lead to one or more persons dominating the activity. The opportunities for piggybacking on ideas are also better with this method, which is sometimes also called freewheeling brainstorming.

Except for the difference in the order in which ideas are launched, the two approaches are identical; the steps for applying them are presented on the next page.

Problem Solving

Root Cause Analysis

Problem Understanding

Problem Cause Brainstorming

Problem Cause Data Collection

Problem Cause Data Analysis

Root Cause Identification

Root Cause Elimination

Solution Implementation

Tool Selection

Example Cases

Problem Solving

Root Cause
Analysis

Problem
Understanding

**Problem Cause
Brainstorming**

Problem Cause
Data Collection

Problem Cause
Data Analysis

Root Cause
Identification

Root Cause
Elimination

Solution
Implementation

Tool Selection

Example Cases

THE STEPS IN BRAINSTORMING

1. Clearly define the topic to brainstorm and write it on top of a whiteboard or a flip-chart.

2. Allow participants to launch ideas according to the approach used, structured or unstructured.

3. Write down every idea launched, using the same wording as the original proposition.

4. Do not discuss, criticize, or evaluate ideas during the session.

5. Allow the flow of ideas to stagnate once, because it will usually pick up again. Close the process when new ideas are only reformulations of previously launched ideas or when few new ideas are evident.

6. Evaluate the ideas by sorting them into groups, either by theme or by decreasing potential.

An Example of the Use of Brainstorming

When many of the receptionists at a large international business hotel realized that it frequently took more time to check their guests in and out than what had been allocated, they initiated a brainstorming session to identify the reasons. One of the managers of the hotel was a member of a group from the hotel chain administration who frequently traveled to many hotels to evaluate their service, and could confirm their considerably lower performance. He and seven receptionists formed the brainstorming team.

They defined the theme of the brainstorming as "reasons we make our guests wait unnecessarily long when checking in and out of our hotel." The freewheeling approach was chosen, and the group started its session an hour before lunch on a Thursday. A group clerk took position by the whiteboard, and the brainstorming went on for about 50 minutes. By that time, 42 ideas had been tabled, though some were closely related or similar. After a break for lunch, the team combined and grouped ideas, eventually sorting them according to their impact on the problem.

Some important ideas that resulted from the brainstorming included: the registration form required more information than was necessary from the guests; the hotel lacked a guest database that could retrieve information for repeat customers; the desk was understaffed during peak hours; the desk staff was required to handle queries about directions, transportation, and so forth; and there were too few credit card company links. Needless to say, these had to be further analyzed, but they represented a very good starting point for ensuing improvement efforts.

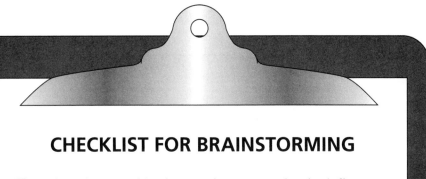

CHECKLIST FOR BRAINSTORMING

❑ Before the actual brainstorming starts, clearly define and communicate to everyone the topic of the session.

❑ Decide which mode of idea launching to use, free-wheeling or round-robin.

❑ Record ideas as they are launched; do not attempt to reformulate or redefine them.

❑ Allow everyone the opportunity (and time) to launch all their ideas.

❑ Do not allow criticism during the idea-generation phase.

❑ Allow the flow of ideas to slow once, then to resume, without terminating the session.

❑ Stop the session when the flow of ideas slows again or new ideas are variants of previously launched concepts.

❑ Evaluate (and possibly reformulate) the ideas.

❑ Combine and group ideas.

If the brainstorming is part of a larger project or process, agree on clear tasks with responsibilities and deadlines to further process the outcome of the brainstorming.

Problem Solving

Root Cause Analysis

Problem Understanding

Problem Cause Brainstorming

Problem Cause Data Collection

Problem Cause Data Analysis

Root Cause Identification

Root Cause Elimination

Solution Implementation

Tool Selection

Example Cases

Problem Solving

Root Cause
Analysis

Problem
Understanding

**Problem Cause
Brainstorming**

Problem Cause
Data Collection

Problem Cause
Data Analysis

Root Cause
Identification

Root Cause
Elimination

Solution
Implementation

Tool Selection

Example Cases

BRAINSTORMING RECORDING TEMPLATE

Brainstorming

Topic:

Participants: **Date:**

Ideas

Idea Groups

THE PURPOSE AND APPLICATIONS OF BRAINWRITING

While brainwriting serves the same purpose as brainstorming, it offers these advantages:

- Everyone has better access to the process.

- Participants can describe more detailed and coherent ideas.

- It is possible to protect the anonymity of the participants, which is useful if you're dealing with a touchy subject.

Typical applications during root cause analysis include generating ideas about problems, consequences, and ways to eliminate causes in situations where:

- Complex ideas are expected.

- It is feared that some people might dominate the brainstorming were it conducted orally.

Two Types of Brainwriting

There are two ways to conduct a brainwriting session. The objective is the same with both approaches and most of the steps are identical; the difference lies in the way ideas are recorded.

- In the card method, ideas are written on small cards and circulated among the participants, who add related ideas or expand on the existing ones.

- In the gallery method, ideas are written on a number of whiteboards or flip-charts and the participants circulate among them, adding related ideas or expanding on the existing ones.

Problem Solving

Root Cause Analysis

Problem Understanding

Problem Cause Brainstorming

Problem Cause Data Collection

Problem Cause Data Analysis

Root Cause Identification

Root Cause Elimination

Solution Implementation

Tool Selection

Example Cases

THE STEPS IN BRAINWRITING

1. As with brainstorming, start by clearly defining the target topic for possible cause brainstorming. Depending on the method used, write the topic:

   • On a whiteboard for the gallery method

   • On participants' individual cards for the card method

2. Have participants write down their ideas on their cards or on the whiteboard. Encourage precise explanations.

3. Allow participants to add to others' ideas to realize the benefits of combining ideas or further developing them.

4. Ask the group to discuss the ideas and, if possible, sort them into classes.

An Example of the Use of Brainwriting

At the hotel described in the brainstorming example, the team that looked at why checking in and out took so long came up with a multitude of possible reasons. Many of these involved more extensive issues that could not possibly be changed by the receptionists themselves, either because they involved large investments or affected the policy and operations of other parts of the hotel.

To take the ideas further and look at possible ways to remedy the situation, a different group was formed. When three receptionists, the general manager, the accountant, and a computer analyst tried to build on the success of the previous brainstorming by using the same approach, the once-creative receptionists seemed repressed and contributed few ideas. It was also apparent that the sole reason behind this change in behavior was the dominating presence of the general manager. The group therefore discarded what had been done during the fruitless brainstorming session and instead conducted a round of brainwriting.

Even though this did not immediately restore the previous creativity of the receptionists, the result was far better. Some good ideas included installing a simple guest database that would provide quick responses when searching for a guest's name, encouraging guests to settle their bills the previous night to allow express checkout in the morning, rethinking manpower use throughout the day to better cover peaks, and placing an "oracle" in the reception area to answer questions not related directly to rooms or accounts.

CHECKLIST FOR BRAINWRITING

❑ Before the brainwriting starts, clearly define and communicate to everyone the topic of the session.

❑ Decide which approach to use, the gallery method or the card method.

❑ Have the individual participants generate and write down ideas.

❑ When everyone has completed the idea generation, have the group try to build on one another's ideas and combine and extend them.

❑ Evaluate (and possibly reformulate) the ideas.

❑ Combine and group ideas.

❑ If the brainwriting is part of a larger project or process, agree on clear tasks with responsibilities and deadlines to further process the outcome of the brainwriting.

Problem Solving

Root Cause Analysis

Problem Understanding

Problem Cause Brainstorming

Problem Cause Data Collection

Problem Cause Data Analysis

Root Cause Identification

Root Cause Elimination

Solution Implementation

Tool Selection

Example Cases

Problem Solving

Root Cause
Analysis

Problem
Understanding

**Problem Cause
Brainstorming**

Problem Cause
Data Collection

Problem Cause
Data Analysis

Root Cause
Identification

Root Cause
Elimination

Solution
Implementation

Tool Selection

Example Cases

BRAINWRITING CARD AND
WHITEBOARD TEMPLATE

Brainwriting

Topic: **Date:**

Individual Ideas

Brainwriting

Topic: **Date:**

Idea Groups

THE PURPOSE AND APPLICATIONS OF
IS–IS NOT MATRICES

When brainstorming a problem and its possible causes, there is a danger of reaching a state of overload, where the ideas are so plentiful that it becomes difficult to separate the essential from the trivial.

The is–is not matrix is a tool that helps us see this distinction and clarify what the problem *is* or *is not* about, for the purpose of:

• Understanding plausible problem causes

• Identifying issues that are definitely not related to the problem

By comparing "is" with "is not," we can more quickly determine which places we need to start looking at more closely.

Matrix Table

Many of the tools and techniques presented have the word *matrix* in their title. From our own university days, we know from calculus that matrix manipulation can involve highly complex operations. Thus, we suspect that people who have been exposed to matrices at some time in their education or elsewhere could be somewhat wary of tools involving a matrix, not to mention those who never learned about them.

We are therefore glad to say that in all the tools and techniques in this book that involve matrices of some sort, the word *matrix* can easily be replaced by *table*. These matrices/tables are primarily ways to arrange textual or numerical information, either for clearer presentation or for conducting some type of analysis. In any case, there is never a question of performing advanced numerical matrix manipulations. So there is no need to fear matrix-based tools; on a whole they are easy to use and often quite powerful.

Problem Solving

Root Cause Analysis

Problem Understanding

Problem Cause Brainstorming

Problem Cause Data Collection

Problem Cause Data Analysis

Root Cause Identification

Root Cause Elimination

Solution Implementation

Tool Selection

Example Cases

THE STEPS IN IS–IS NOT MATRICES

1. Create an empty matrix of six rows by four columns (or start from the template on p. 57) and fill the header column with the standard headings shown in the template.

2. In the upper left corner of the matrix, state the problem being analyzed.

3. Fill in the second column with "is" information; what is affected, where, when, who, and so on.

4. In the same way, fill in the third column with "is not" information.

5. Compare the two columns for anything odd or that stands out and place these in the fourth column.

6. For each element in this column, analyze how it could be a cause of the problem.

7. For the possible causes identified this way, test them by checking if they explain all items in the "is" and "is not" columns. The/those that do are likely the real cause(s).

An Example of the Use of Is–Is Not Matrix

A real estate agent relied heavily on using the Internet for the marketing of properties for sale, adding both factual information, technical tests, pictures, and even video to each prospect. This was highly effective in attracting potential buyers and much appreciated by them, as they could browse properties from their own desk at home.

After having used this approach for several months, and having expanded the service considerably, among other ways by adding more video clips, more and more complaints were registered from both sellers and buyers. They complained that the prospect information did not show up correctly, more specifically that video clips would not be play.

Having trouble understanding what caused these apparently random problems, and losing some of the company's good reputation because of them, a small team decided to try compiling an is–is not matrix to see if this would help them.

The resulting matrix is shown on the next page. When reviewing the matrix and a list of the prospects with errors, one of the persons responsible for compiling the prospects and publishing them on the Web realized that all the errors occurred in prospects stored on one of two Web servers used.

Continued

Continued

As storage space needs had increased, expecially because of adding video clips, a new Web server had been installed to supplement the old one, but running slightly different software. The team suspected that the problem was with the new server's software.

An IT expert soon confirmed that the way the Web pages were designed caused some problems, especially for video streaming, on the new server. Changing the software to the same as on the old server eliminated all problems.

Problem Solving

Root Cause Analysis

Problem Understanding

Problem Cause Brainstorming

Problem Cause Data Collection

Problem Cause Data Analysis

Root Cause Identification

Root Cause Elimination

Solution Implementation

Tool Selection

Example Cases

IS–IS NOT MATRIX EXAMPLE—REAL ESTATE AGENT

Problem: *Web prospect errors*	Is	Is Not	Distinctions
What occurs, what objects are affected?	Video clips do not play	Other types of information show up correctly	Only video clips have problems
Where does the problem occur?	Web prospects stored on new server	Web prospects stored on old server	No problems on old server
When does the problem occur?	Reported randomly	Not dependent on time of day or week	
Extent of problems	Increasing amount of complaints from both property sellers and buyers	Covering all Web prospects	
Who is involved?	Editor of Web prospects	Sales agents	Not related to input from sales agents

Problem Solving

Root Cause
Analysis

Problem
Understanding

**Problem Cause
Brainstorming**

Problem Cause
Data Collection

Problem Cause
Data Analysis

Root Cause
Identification

Root Cause
Elimination

Solution
Implementation

Tool Selection

Example Cases

CHECKLIST FOR IS–IS NOT MATRICES

❑ Create an empty matrix with six rows and four columns and the appropriate headings.

❑ Fill the header column with the standard headings shown in the template.

❑ Clearly define the problem and place it in the upper left corner of the matrix.

❑ Brainstorm and formulate precisely elements in the "is" and "is not" columns.

❑ Consider whether there are elements in the "is not" column that could have been expected to occur but did not.

❑ Fill in the "distinction" column by comparing the "is" and "is not" columns.

❑ If the matrix was filled in and no likely cause emerged, revisit the matrix to generate more elements.

IS–IS NOT MATRIX TEMPLATE

Problem:	Is	Is Not	Distinctions
What occurs, what objects are affected?			
Where does the problem occur?			
When does the problem occur?			
Extent of problems			
Who is involved?			

Problem Solving

Root Cause Analysis

Problem Understanding

Problem Cause Brainstorming

Problem Cause Data Collection

Problem Cause Data Analysis

Root Cause Identification

Root Cause Elimination

Solution Implementation

Tool Selection

Example Cases

Problem Solving

Root Cause
Analysis

Problem
Understanding

**Problem Cause
Brainstorming**

Problem Cause
Data Collection

Problem Cause
Data Analysis

Root Cause
Identification

Root Cause
Elimination

Solution
Implementation

Tool Selection

Example Cases

THE PURPOSE AND APPLICATIONS OF NOMINAL GROUP TECHNIQUE (NGT)

When brainstorming, the loudest person or persons can sometimes dominate the activity. While discussing ideas, these people will generally continue to dominate, which can cause the group to arrive at minority decisions.

The nominal group technique can facilitate a form of brainstorming in which all participants have the same vote when selecting solutions.

Typical root cause analysis applications are:

• Generating ideas by tapping the entire group's potential

• Gaining consensus about which ideas to pursue further throughout the analysis

---

What Is Consensus?

Consensus is a somewhat tricky concept that is often believed to mean that absolutely everyone involved in a decision must agree if it is to be a consensus decision. Fortunately, this is not the case. According to Webster's dictionary, consensus means, "The judgment arrived at by most of those concerned."

Obtaining full agreement from every person in a group is often impossible, so only a majority of those with a vote in the matter need to agree. This makes life much simpler in regard to root cause analysis, which is based on a joint undertaking by a group and involves creativity and decisions along the way.

When the group votes on an issue and the majority favors one option, consensus has been achieved and the group can move on. If the rules of consensus have been made clear to the group at the outset, such majority decisions should cause no tension, as everyone knows they must be abided by.

Another aspect of consensus is accepting decisions that have been made. All too often we see attempts at starting rematches about conclusions reached, thus disrupting the pursuit of decisions already taken. This is not only impolite toward those behind the consensus decision, but also time-consuming and an obstacle to effective implementation. In team settings, such behavior should be avoided.

THE STEPS IN NOMINAL GROUP TECHNIQUE

1. Each person generates ideas and writes them on idea cards, one idea on each card.

2. The session leader assigns each idea a letter (from A onward) and registers it on a flip-chart. Participants briefly discuss the ideas for clarification and elimination of similar ideas.

3. Participants individually rank the ideas on their ranking card by selecting up to five ideas and assigning points to them, from 5 for the most important/best idea down to 1 for the least important/ good idea.

4. The session leader collects the ranking cards and totals the points.

5. The idea achieving the highest total score is the group's prioritized idea or solution, and will be the logical starting point for the ensuing activities in the root cause analysis.

An Example of the Use of Nominal Group Technique

A medium-sized high school faced some severe problems with bullying and generally unacceptable behavior, though not only among the students. During the last few years, a number of skilled teachers had left the school due to the poor work climate among the employees. A task force of five teachers, two students, one custodial worker, and one administrator was assembled to look into the problems.

The team soon discovered that there were immense differences in opinion as to what caused the low job satisfaction, and the different groups of people tended to blame the others. After a few weeks of fruitless discussions, the task force was no closer to solving the problems, let alone agreeing on their causes. To move the job forward, they agreed to try the nominal group technique.

There was no lack of ideas for possible causes and these had been recorded in minutes from the meetings held so far. These were narrowed to a smaller group to be voted on, and a list with assigned letters was produced, as shown on the top of the following page. Below the idea list, one teacher's ranking card is depicted. Finally, the resulting total scores for the different ideas are shown at the bottom of the page. From this exercise, the task force was able to move on, concentrating on the four highest-ranked consensus ideas: 1) the isolation of the job, 2) time pressures, 3) the lack of activities of a social nature, and 4) the appearance of the school building and facilities.

Problem Solving

Root Cause Analysis

Problem Understanding

Problem Cause Brainstorming

Problem Cause Data Collection

Problem Cause Data Analysis

Root Cause Identification

Root Cause Elimination

Solution Implementation

Tool Selection

Example Cases

Problem Solving

Root Cause Analysis

Problem Understanding

Problem Cause Brainstorming

Problem Cause Data Collection

Problem Cause Data Analysis

Root Cause Identification

Root Cause Elimination

Solution Implementation

Tool Selection

Example Cases

A. People simply do not know one another
B. There are no social arrangements
C. People don't care about other people
D. The staff takes after the students, but makes everything more serious **[QU AU: Unclear]**
E. The school looks so sloppy, there are no incentives for behaving any better
F. Too much work and too little time to do it
G. The teachers look down on the other employees
H. Manners are neglected
I. Everyone works alone, there are no tasks requiring a collective effort
J. Too many aggressive young males
K. Competition for pay raises fosters a cold atmosphere

Ranking Card NGT

Problem: Bad work climate in school

Idea	Points
F	5
K	4
I	1
A	2
D	3

Nominal Group Technique

Problem: Bad work climate in school

Idea	Points	Total
A	2 3 1	6
B	4 5 1 2	12
C	1 1 5	7
D	2 2 3 1	8
E	4 4 3	11
F	5 5 4 5 1	20
G	2 3	5
H	2 3	5
I	5 5 4 3 4	21
J	1 2	3
K	3 4	7

CHECKLIST FOR NOMINAL GROUP TECHNIQUE

❑ Before the possible cause brainstorming is started, clearly define and communicate to everyone the topic of the session.

❑ Select a session leader.

❑ Distribute idea cards to the participants.

❑ Individual participants generate ideas and write them down on their idea cards.

❑ When everyone has completed the idea generation, write the ideas on a whiteboard or flip-chart and assign each a letter.

❑ Discuss the ideas to clarify vague entries and eliminate similar ones.

❑ Have the participants individually and without any influence from others rank the ideas using their ranking cards.

❑ Have the session leader collect the cards and total the scores for all ideas.

❑ Accept the highest-ranking ideas as the group's consensus solution.

Problem Solving

Root Cause Analysis

Problem Understanding

Problem Cause Brainstorming

Problem Cause Data Collection

Problem Cause Data Analysis

Root Cause Identification

Root Cause Elimination

Solution Implementation

Tool Selection

Example Cases

NOMINAL GROUP TECHNIQUE IDEA AND RANKING CARDS

Ranking Card NGT

Problem:

Idea	Points

Nominal Group Technique

Problem:

Idea	Points	Total
A		
B		
C		
D		
E		
F		
G		
H		
I		
J		
K		

THE PURPOSE AND APPLICATIONS OF PAIRED COMPARISONS

The ideas available for voting on might be many and the ideas may vary. In such situations, it can be difficult to decide which idea to vote for, and the results might be determined by coincidence.

Like the other tools described in this chapter, paired comparisons aims at prioritization and consensus reaching, but does so through a sequence of paired comparisons. One-to-one decisions are easier to make than selecting among a large number of possible solutions.

Typical applications of paired comparisons include:

- Prioritizing different alternative problems or causes

- Helping decisions surface when there are many alternatives

Methods Similar to Paired Comparisons

There are other methods that also rely on the basic idea of prioritizing among two or more ideas or elements to end up with a ranked list. While these might work just as well as paired comparisons or nominal group technique, they are often more complex without necessarily adding benefits. Some such methods you might want to consider are:

- *Balance sheet.* A simple tool where pros and cons of the alternative ideas are listed in an effort to clarify what each entails.

- *Criteria rating form* (sometimes called criteria testing). A numerical approach for applying certain evaluation criteria to a set of ideas in order to choose among them.

- *Weighted voting.* A method similar to nominal group technique.

Problem Solving

Root Cause Analysis

Problem Understanding

Problem Cause Brainstorming

Problem Cause Data Collection

Problem Cause Data Analysis

Root Cause Identification

Root Cause Elimination

Solution Implementation

Tool Selection

Example Cases

Problem Solving

Root Cause
Analysis

Problem
Understanding

**Problem Cause
Brainstorming**

Problem Cause
Data Collection

Problem Cause
Data Analysis

Root Cause
Identification

Root Cause
Elimination

Solution
Implementation

Tool Selection

Example Cases

THE STEPS IN PAIRED COMPARISONS

1. Clearly identify the alternatives to be compared. The total number, denoted *N*, should be manageable, that is, not more than eight.

2. Create a matrix with the alternatives, coded by letters, as row headings and the pairs as column headings, indicated by letters only to save space. The number of pairs *p* is determined by the following formula:

$$p = [N \times (N - 1)]/2$$

3. Column by column, each participant votes for one of the alternatives; the votes are logged in the matrix.

4. After all participants have voted for all pairs, sum the total number for each pair; this should equal the number of participants.

5. Sum the number of votes cast for each alternative to give the row totals. The highest-scoring alternative is the preferred one according to the group.

An Example of the Use of Paired Comparisons

A large car dealer had been in the same perfect downtown location, in terms of customer availability, for years. This particular location also generated problems though, especially for the repair shop. Having very little space available, it was difficult to park cars that were waiting to be serviced or picked up. Customers often waited up to an hour to get their cars out of the lot.

Although it would be impossible to do something about the available space, the two foremen and five mechanics put their heads together to look into the primary reasons why customers were kept waiting. After brainstorming among themselves and soliciting ideas from their coworkers, they narrowed the list down to the one shown on the following page.

However, when trying to decide which of these factors were contributing most to the problem, thus prioritizing which to attack first, major disagreements surfaced. Following heated debate, on the verge of developing into a physical fight, the manager of the dealership suggested they use paired comparisons to arrive at a conclusion.

The mechanics designed a matrix on their whiteboard and went through the entire voting procedure, as shown on the bottom of the next page. Working from this, they implemented a system in which magnetic boxes containing the vehicle keys were attached to the roof of each car in the parking lot. The boxes could be removed only by using a remote control, which every mechanic was furnished, ensuring that whenever a car had to be moved, the keys were readily available to do so.

PAIRED COMPARISONS EXAMPLE—
CAR DEALER

A. No system for parking cars in the order in which they will be retrieved

B. Some people park in a way that requires much more space than necessary

C. Whenever a car needs to be moved, the keys are impossible to find

D. The gate from the lot to the repair shop is too narrow

E. Too many cars are accepted each day, resulting in some of them having to stay parked overnight

	A/B	A/C	A/D	A/E	B/C	B/D	B/E	C/D	C/E	D/E	Total
A	5	2	3	3							13
B	2				1	4	5				12
C		5			6			6	5		22
D			4			3		1		4	12
E				4			2		2	3	11
Number of votes	7	7	7	7	7	7	7	7	7	7	

Problem Solving

Root Cause Analysis

Problem Understanding

Problem Cause Brainstorming

Problem Cause Data Collection

Problem Cause Data Analysis

Root Cause Identification

Root Cause Elimination

Solution Implementation

Tool Selection

Example Cases

Problem Solving

Root Cause
Analysis

Problem
Understanding

**Problem Cause
Brainstorming**

Problem Cause
Data Collection

Problem Cause
Data Analysis

Root Cause
Identification

Root Cause
Elimination

Solution
Implementation

Tool Selection

Example Cases

CHECKLIST FOR PAIRED COMPARISONS

❏ Before the paired comparison starts, generate a list of alternatives—for example, through brainstorming or brainwriting.

❏ Reduce the list of alternatives to a number that can be practically handled in the comparison session, that is, not more than eight.

❏ Determine the number of pairs and design a matrix.

❏ Have each participant vote for the pairs, column by column, in the matrix; log the votes.

❏ Control that the number of votes cast add up by summing the total number of votes for each pair.

❏ In case of discrepancies in the number of votes, revote the pairs in dispute.

❏ Sum the grand totals for each alternative.

❏ The alternative receiving the highest number of votes is declared the consensus decision.

PAIRED COMPARISONS TEMPLATE

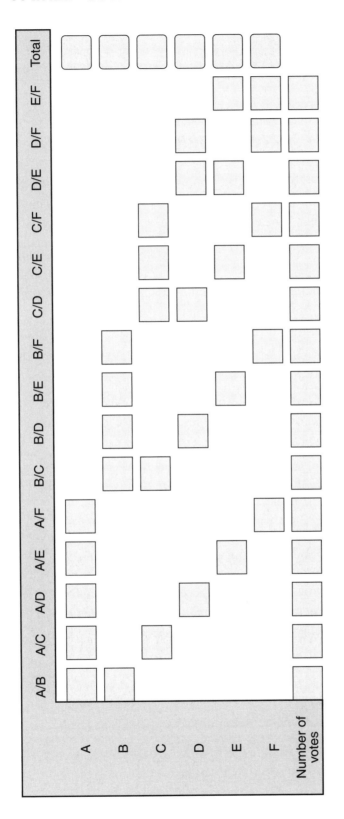

Problem Solving

Root Cause Analysis

Problem Understanding

Problem Cause Brainstorming

Problem Cause Data Collection

Problem Cause Data Analysis

Root Cause Identification

Root Cause Elimination

Solution Implementation

Tool Selection

Example Cases

Problem Solving

Root Cause
Analysis

Problem
Understanding

**Problem Cause
Brainstorming**

Problem Cause
Data Collection

Problem Cause
Data Analysis

Root Cause
Identification

Root Cause
Elimination

Solution
Implementation

Tool Selection

Example Cases

PROBLEM CAUSE BRAINSTORMING CHECKLIST

Although root cause analysis is not one clear process from start to finish, some distinct stages in the analysis are discernible. This checklist helps assess whether the most important elements of the problem cause brainstorming stage have been accomplished before moving on.

❑ Decide which problem needs possible cause brainstorming and clearly define the objective of the session. Typical applications include generating ideas about which problem to solve, possible causes for a problem, and possible solutions to a problem.

❑ Assess the situation in which the possible cause brainstorming will take place to select a suitable approach. Typical considerations include allowing everyone to participate properly, anonymity, complexity, and so on. Tools to choose between are brainstorming, brainwriting, and the is–is not matrix.

❑ After idea generation is completed, decide if prioritization of the ideas is necessary. If so, assess whether this could be accomplished by analyzing the entire set of ideas. The purpose of this assessment is to select between nominal group technique or paired comparisons.

❑ Reach a consensus on the prioritization of the ideas by using one of these techniques. The consensus solution is taken to the problem cause data collection stage.

5

Tools for Problem Cause Data Collection

Problem Solving

Root Cause Analysis

Problem Understanding

Problem Cause Brainstorming

Problem Cause Data Collection

Problem Cause Data Analysis

Root Cause Identification

Root Cause Elimination

Solution Implementation

Tool Selection

Example Cases

This chapter contains a selection of tools and techniques that you can use to collect data during root cause analysis. Typically, these tools and techniques are used in conjunction with many of the other tools in this book.

Problem Solving

Root Cause
Analysis

Problem
Understanding

Problem Cause
Brainstorming

**Problem Cause
Data Collection**

Problem Cause
Data Analysis

Root Cause
Identification

Root Cause
Elimination

Solution
Implementation

Tool Selection

Example Cases

PROBLEM CAUSE DATA COLLECTION

One important distinction between haphazard problem solving and structured root cause analysis is the extent to which data are collected and used. While the former tends to result in "shots in the dark," analysis based on insight *and* facts has a much better chance of accomplishing its objectives.

Thus, systematic collection of valid and reliable data is an important activity in root cause analysis.

The tools that can be used for this purpose are:

• Sampling

• Surveys

• Check sheet

Collect a Representative Set of Data

After receiving a complaint letter from a customer, the manager of a small restaurant changed both the menu and the practice of allowing guests to reserve tables. The complaining customer wanted a wider selection of appetizers, main courses, and desserts and did not like the fact that when he visited the restaurant, there often were no tables available.

After having made changes according to this customer's wishes, the business gradually declined. People who previously dined there several times a week were highly displeased with the changes that had been made and now only came by occasionally. Had the proprietor collected a representative set of data earlier, instead of acting on the single complaint, this costly experience could have been avoided.

THE PURPOSE AND APPLICATIONS OF SAMPLING

During root cause analysis, it is often necessary to collect data about the problem and its possible causes. Collecting data might take a long time, be costly, or require a lot of effort. Sampling is a way of economizing the data-collection process.

The main purpose of sampling is to draw conclusions about a larger group based on a smaller sample, as long as you are aware of the sample's limitations.

Applications in root cause analysis include:

- Effectively collecting data about problems or causes

- Gaining a better understanding of the situation

Types of Sampling

Sampling is a collective term that encompasses several approaches to the cost- and time-efficient collection of data. Some of the most common types of sampling include:

- *Random sampling.* Random numbers are used to determine which units will be drawn from a larger population. Random numbers can be found in special tables, by using a computer to generate them, or simply by throwing dice. An example is pulling out numbers 4, 11, 19, 21, 34, and so on, for testing for defects.

- *Systematic sampling.* A means to overcome the fact that random sampling can at times be difficult or even impossible. In systematic sampling, measures are made at fixed intervals of time, numbers, length, and so on. For example, every 20 minutes, the number of customers waiting in line are counted.

- *Stratified sampling.* A necessary tool when you know that there are differences between categories within the entire population. In such situations, data is purposely collected from each of the categories so that the samples represent the categories in the right proportions to one another. If a company has seven salespeople, customer satisfaction scores can be collected from the customers of each, relative to the number of customers each serves.

- *Cluster sampling.* An adequate approach when the population is known to be stable and without much variation. In this case, a group of the units is taken to represent the whole population—for example, the entire batch of parts produced during an hour may represent an entire week's production.

Problem Solving

Root Cause Analysis

Problem Understanding

Problem Cause Brainstorming

Problem Cause Data Collection

Problem Cause Data Analysis

Root Cause Identification

Root Cause Elimination

Solution Implementation

Tool Selection

Example Cases

Problem Solving

Root Cause
Analysis

Problem
Understanding

Problem Cause
Brainstorming

**Problem Cause
Data Collection**

Problem Cause
Data Analysis

Root Cause
Identification

Root Cause
Elimination

Solution
Implementation

Tool Selection

Example Cases

THE STEPS IN USING SAMPLING

Unlike most of the other tools presented here, sampling is not one unified tool where the steps can easily be outlined. Rather, sampling is used to support other tools. Some important issues to keep in mind:

- Assess the nature of the population to be sampled to decide on a suitable type of sampling approach (take into account the homogeneity of the population, any clustering of data, and so on).

- Collect the sample of data according to the chosen sampling approach.

- By calculating simple figures such as averages, means, and so on, you can test whether the sample is a reasonable representation of the population.

An Example of the Use of Sampling

Customers of a manufacturer of ballpoint pens used for promotions frequently complained because many of the pens didn't work or stopped working after a relatively short time. The pens' recipients transferred this same level of quality to their view of the companies giving them away.

The pens were manufactured in seven different manufacturing lines. To determine if the quality varied among these lines, the company wanted to undertake a random quality control assessment of the finished products. However, to ensure that the same data were collected from all seven lines, the company needed to introduce a systematic sampling procedure: for one week, they collected the first three pens produced each hour from each of the seven lines. Each pen was tested immediately and again after having been used for one minute.

The data showed clear differences between the manufacturing lines. Five lines produced pens of adequate quality, while two others generated close to 95 percent of the defective product. After these stunning results, the next step was to start looking for the causes of these high defect rates, which is a different story.

CHECKLIST FOR SAMPLING

❑ Before sampling, assess the sample population to ensure that a suitable sampling method is being used.

❑ During the sampling, collect data in accordance with the chosen sampling analysis approach.

❑ After a period of sampling, ensure that the sample does, in fact, represent an accurate picture of the entire population.

Problem Solving

Root Cause Analysis

Problem Understanding

Problem Cause Brainstorming

Problem Cause Data Collection

Problem Cause Data Analysis

Root Cause Identification

Root Cause Elimination

Solution Implementation

Tool Selection

Example Cases

Problem Solving

Root Cause
Analysis

Problem
Understanding

Problem Cause
Brainstorming

**Problem Cause
Data Collection**

Problem Cause
Data Analysis

Root Cause
Identification

Root Cause
Elimination

Solution
Implementation

Tool Selection

Example Cases

A Few Words on Sample Size

Even after deciding on a type of sampling, you still need to answer two important questions:

- How many samples need to be collected?

- What is the preferred size of the samples?

There is no simple way to answer these two questions, but there are some factors that impact the decisions, including:

- Whether the collected data will be discrete—that is, correct/wrong, yes/no, and so on—or continuous—that is, measurable in inches, pounds, volts, and so on

- The size of the total population

- How difficult it will be to collect the data

- How costly it will be to collect the data

- The expected level of variation in the sampled population

- What the consequences of inaccurate samples could be

Depending on the purpose of the sampling, there are also standards available that specify sample size and frequency. Such standards are available both as military standards, ANSI standards, and ISO standards. For a list of relevant standards, see for example http://www.variation.com/techlib/standard.html.

THE PURPOSE AND APPLICATIONS OF SURVEYS

The data mentioned in the example of the use of sampling were quantitative and easily measured. When you want to collect data about people's attitudes, feelings, or opinions, an additional instrument is useful, namely a survey. Surveys are helpful when collecting such data.

The main purpose of surveys is to collect data from respondents.

In root cause analysis, the most common uses of surveys include:

- Collecting customer satisfaction data related to a problem

- Determining customer needs and expectations

Ways of Conducting Surveys

First, a survey is a structured data collection session that requires a pre-defined set of questions. These questions are normally contained in a questionnaire developed for the survey.

Second, there are at least two different ways to solicit answers to the questions from the respondents in the survey, including:

- Having the respondents complete the questionnaire in writing, either on paper or electronically.

- Conducting an interview with the respondent and letting the interviewer fill in the answers. Such interviews can be performed over the phone or through personal contact.

With all surveys, large amounts of data can be collected relatively easily and inexpensively. While questionnaires filled in by the respondents generate the most data per dollar, interviews tend to give data of higher quality.

Problem Solving

Root Cause Analysis

Problem Understanding

Problem Cause Brainstorming

Problem Cause Data Collection

Problem Cause Data Analysis

Root Cause Identification

Root Cause Elimination

Solution Implementation

Tool Selection

Example Cases

Problem Solving

Root Cause
Analysis

Problem
Understanding

Problem Cause
Brainstorming

**Problem Cause
Data Collection**

Problem Cause
Data Analysis

Root Cause
Identification

Root Cause
Elimination

Solution
Implementation

Tool Selection

Example Cases

THE STEPS IN USING SURVEYS

1. Clearly define the objective of the survey and how the data will be used later.

2. Determine what information is required to achieve this objective.

3. Decide how the survey will be undertaken—that is, written (via mail, fax, e-mail, or the Internet) or verbal (by telephone or in person).

4. Develop the questionnaire, keeping in mind issues such as type and sequence of questions, understandability, language, grouping of questions, brevity, and so on.

5. Test the questionnaire to ensure that all questions are easy to understand and can measure what they are intended to.

6. Identify the sample of respondents.

7. Perform the survey according to the chosen approach.

An Example of the Use of a Survey

A computer store had specialized in selling to first-time unskilled buyers, some of whom were touching a computer for the first time. Many of the customers required a lot of support and technical guidance during the first few weeks after the purchase, and many customers complained about their buying experience.

To determine what caused these problems, the store developed a customer satisfaction survey; they sent a simple questionnaire (shown on the following page) to every buyer six weeks after the purchase, along with a return envelope with prepaid postage. To encourage people to return the questionnaire, a drawing for $1,000 in software among those who returned the questionnaire was held after four months.

The survey yielded about 150 completed questionnaires. After company officials assembled and analyzed the data, the cause of most of the dissatisfaction became clear.

CUSTOMER SATISFACTION SURVEY EXAMPLE—COMPUTER STORE

To improve our service to you, we are conducting a short survey on your experiences in buying a computer from us. We would greatly appreciate your taking time to fill in the questionnaire.

Please indicate your responses by checking the appropriate boxes.

	Poor					Excellent
	1	2	3	4	5	6

1. Overall, how would you rate your purchase from our store? ❑ ❑ ❑ ❑ ❑ ❑

2. How would you rate the following aspects of our service:

   Computer hardware and accessories selection? ❑ ❑ ❑ ❑ ❑ ❑

   Hardware and accessories prices? ❑ ❑ ❑ ❑ ❑ ❑

   Software selection? ❑ ❑ ❑ ❑ ❑ ❑

   Software prices? ❑ ❑ ❑ ❑ ❑ ❑

   Salesperson's knowledge and ability to help you? ❑ ❑ ❑ ❑ ❑ ❑

   Delivery time of the equipment you bought? ❑ ❑ ❑ ❑ ❑ ❑

   Quality of the instructions and manuals? ❑ ❑ ❑ ❑ ❑ ❑

   Technical support during installation? ❑ ❑ ❑ ❑ ❑ ❑

   Technical support after first installation? ❑ ❑ ❑ ❑ ❑ ❑

   Reliability of the equipment? ❑ ❑ ❑ ❑ ❑ ❑

3. Would you recommend our store to others? ❑ Yes ❑ No

4. What is your age? ❑ <30 ❑ >30

5. What is your gender? ❑ Male ❑ Female

Thank you very much!

Problem Solving

Root Cause Analysis

Problem Understanding

Problem Cause Brainstorming

Problem Cause Data Collection

Problem Cause Data Analysis

Root Cause Identification

Root Cause Elimination

Solution Implementation

Tool Selection

Example Cases

Problem Solving

Root Cause
Analysis

Problem
Understanding

Problem Cause
Brainstorming

**Problem Cause
Data Collection**

Problem Cause
Data Analysis

Root Cause
Identification

Root Cause
Elimination

Solution
Implementation

Tool Selection

Example Cases

CHECKLIST FOR SURVEYS

❑ The objective of the survey must be clearly identified before preparing the survey.

❑ Identify the type and amount of data required.

❑ Evaluate possible survey methods and select a suitable approach.

❑ Consider how the collected data will be analyzed, keeping in mind which analysis tools will be used.

❑ Design the questionnaire so the layout fits the objective of the survey, the data to be collected, and the analysis approach selected.

❑ Pretest the questionnaire internally before using it, to adjust and improve both the structure and the questions.

❑ Identify the sample of survey respondents.

❑ Conduct the survey according to the selected approach.

❑ Analyze the collected data using the defined analysis methods.

THE PURPOSE AND APPLICATIONS OF CHECK SHEETS

Data collection can often become an unstructured and messy exercise. A check sheet is a table or a form used to systematically register data as it is collected.

The main purpose of a check sheet is to ensure that all data is registered correctly.

Main applications include:

- Registering how often different problems occur

- Registering the frequency of incidents that are believed to cause problems

---

What Data Is Needed in Root Cause Analysis

Data is a word that sounds very formal—"data is used by bureaucratic governmental institutions and by computers; in the practical world of root cause analysis and problem solving, there is no need for data."

This is the view of many people working with root cause analysis. However, one simple definition of the data is:

"A collection of facts from which conclusions may be drawn."

Isn't this exactly what we need in root cause analysis? As you will see throughout this book, a multitude of different inputs is essential for a good analysis. This input is called data, and it takes many shapes and forms.

Typical types of data that are used in root cause analysis include:

- Events that occur

- The frequency of events

- Errors or defects discovered in products or services

- How long different tasks take to perform

- The costs of certain aspects of a process

Problem Solving

Root Cause Analysis

Problem Understanding

Problem Cause Brainstorming

Problem Cause Data Collection

Problem Cause Data Analysis

Root Cause Identification

Root Cause Elimination

Solution Implementation

Tool Selection

Example Cases

Problem Solving

Root Cause
Analysis

Problem
Understanding

Problem Cause
Brainstorming

**Problem Cause
Data Collection**

Problem Cause
Data Analysis

Root Cause
Identification

Root Cause
Elimination

Solution
Implementation

Tool Selection

Example Cases

THE STEPS IN USING CHECK SHEETS

1. Clearly define what events are to be recorded. (Add a category of "other" to capture incidents not easily categorized into any of the specified groups.)

2. Define the period for data recording and suitable intervals.

3. Design the check sheet to be used during data recording, allocating space for recording each event, and for summarizing within the intervals and the entire recording period.

4. Perform the data collection during the agreed period, ensuring that everyone understands the tasks and events to be recorded.

5. Analyze the data to identify events with unusually few or many occurrences.

An Example of the Use of a Check Sheet

A bookstore located in a large shopping mall consistently achieved lower sales per day than budgeted. The staff noticed that quite a few customers came into the store to browse but left without buying anything. When considering this problem (not tapping the customer base potential), a wide range of possible causes surfaced, including:

- The customers did not find what they were looking for.
- The staff did not offer the necessary help.
- Sought items were temporarily sold out.
- Sought items were not carried by the store.
- Prices were too high.
- There was too long a line at the checkout counter.
- Certain types of credit cards were not accepted.
- Lighting was poor in some areas of the store.
- There were no places to sit and look through books before deciding to buy.

The difficulty of identifying the actual problem and how often it occurred made it difficult for the store personnel to implement any changes. Thus, during a two-week period, many of the customers leaving without making any purchases were courteously asked why this happened. The responses were logged on a check sheet, shown on the following page, and gave a much clearer idea of where to start to improve the situation.

CHECK SHEET EXAMPLE—BOOKSTORE

Cause of no purchase	Week 1	Week 2	Total number of occurrences per cause
Could not find item	⦀⦀⦀ III	⦀⦀⦀⦀	38
No offer of help	⦀⦀ II	⦀ I	18
Item sold out	II	III	5
Item not carried	III	⦀ I	9
Prices too high	I		1
Line too long	I	III	4
Wrong credit cards	II		2
Poor lighting	⦀ II	⦀⦀ II	19
No place to sit	II	IIII	6
Total number of causes per week	48	53	101

Problem Solving

Root Cause Analysis

Problem Understanding

Problem Cause Brainstorming

Problem Cause Data Collection

Problem Cause Data Analysis

Root Cause Identification

Root Cause Elimination

Solution Implementation

Tool Selection

Example Cases

Do Not Let the Check Sheet Make You Overlook Causes

When recommending the use of check sheets during data collection in root cause analysis, a word of warning is appropriate. If the categories of events you are recording in the data collection period have been meticulously defined and inserted into the check sheet, other significant occurrences might often be overlooked.

One way of reducing the risk of making this mistake is to add a category termed "other," in which you can place everything that seems prudent to record but does not fit into one of the other categories. If "other" occurs frequently, make a note. There might be one or two categories that recur often and deserve to be added to the sheet as a specific category.

Problem Solving

Root Cause
Analysis

Problem
Understanding

Problem Cause
Brainstorming

**Problem Cause
Data Collection**

Problem Cause
Data Analysis

Root Cause
Identification

Root Cause
Elimination

Solution
Implementation

Tool Selection

Example Cases

CHECKLIST FOR CHECK SHEETS

❑ Clearly define the events to be recorded on the check sheet to avoid inappropriate registration.

❑ Determine the data collection period.

❑ If the collection period is lengthy, divide it into suitable intervals.

❑ Draw up the check sheet to allow ample space for recording each category.

❑ Collect data during the entire collection period, emphasizing accurate registration.

❑ Total the occurrences in each category for each collection interval and for the entire period.

❑ Identify the most frequently occurring categories.

❑ Note anomalies, for example, events not occurring at all, very infrequently, or in patterns.

CHECK SHEET TEMPLATE

Problem	Period 1	Period 2	Period 3	Total number of occurrences per problem
Total number of problems per period				

Problem Solving

Root Cause Analysis

Problem Understanding

Problem Cause Brainstorming

Problem Cause Data Collection

Problem Cause Data Analysis

Root Cause Identification

Root Cause Elimination

Solution Implementation

Tool Selection

Example Cases

Problem Solving

Root Cause
Analysis

Problem
Understanding

Problem Cause
Brainstorming

**Problem Cause
Data Collection**

Problem Cause
Data Analysis

Root Cause
Identification

Root Cause
Elimination

Solution
Implementation

Tool Selection

Example Cases

PROBLEM CAUSE DATA COLLECTION CHECKLIST

Root cause analysis is not one clear process from start to finish, yet some distinct stages in the analysis are discernible. This checklist should help you assess whether the most important elements of the problem cause data collection stage have been accomplished before moving on.

❑ Use a problem and its possible causes, based on the outcome of problem cause brainstorming, as the starting point of the problem cause data collection stage.

❑ Assess the situation for which data will be collected and determine which tool to use.

❑ When selecting a tool, consider the amount of data needed, the nature of the population, the costs involved, and so on.

❑ Choose among the following approaches: check sheet, sampling, and surveys.

❑ Collect data using the chosen approach, emphasizing accuracy and validity of the data.

❑ The collected data forms the basis for further investigation in the problem understanding stage.

6

Tools for Problem Cause Data Analysis

Problem Solving

Root Cause Analysis

Problem Understanding

Problem Cause Brainstorming

Problem Cause Data Collection

Problem Cause Data Analysis

Root Cause Identification

Root Cause Elimination

Solution Implementation

Tool Selection

Example Cases

In Chapter 6, we present six approaches for analyzing how different possible causes can impact the original problem.

Problem Solving

Root Cause
Analysis

Problem
Understanding

Problem Cause
Brainstorming

Problem Cause
Data Collection

**Problem Cause
Data Analysis**

Root Cause
Identification

Root Cause
Elimination

Solution
Implementation

Tool Selection

Example Cases

PROBLEM CAUSE DATA ANALYSIS

How are the possible causes connected to the problem, and which causes seem to do the most harm? The purpose of the problem cause data analysis phase, the last preparatory stage before attempting to solve the problem, is to clarify possible causes.

The tools available for problem cause data analysis include:

- Histogram

- Pareto chart

- Scatter chart

- Problem concentration diagram

- Relations diagram

- Affinity diagram

It Is Tempting to Charge Ahead

At this point in the root cause analysis, you have completed much preparatory work. Having already generated a list of suspects, it is often tempting to charge ahead and try to solve the problem in one fell swoop by attacking all its possible causes. If you have already reached this point, be patient.

If you chase after all possible causes, you will probably spend too much energy, time, and money eliminating symptoms and lower-level causes— perhaps even the root cause itself. Still, you'll be better off doing more analysis to precisely target the root cause before starting the elimination process.

So be patient, go the last mile, and find the root cause!

THE PURPOSE AND APPLICATIONS OF HISTOGRAMS

A histogram, also called a bar chart, is used to display the distribution and variation of a data set. The data can be measures of length, diameter, duration, costs, attitudes, and so on.

The main purpose of the histogram is to clarify the presentation of data. You can present the same information in a table; however, the graphic presentation format usually makes it easier to see relationships.

Typical applications of histograms in root cause analysis include:

- Presenting data to determine which causes dominate

- Understanding the distribution of occurrences of different problems, causes, consequences, and so on

---

The Normal Distribution of Data Points

In the discussion of histograms, it is important to mention a basic statistical concept—namely, the normal distribution.

If you were to measure the time it takes to get to work each morning, you would probably focus on one value: the most likely duration of the trip. When a set of observations is distributed evenly around such a center point, or expected value, statisticians use *normal distribution* to describe these observations and calculate various likelihoods. If data from a normal distribution is presented in a histogram, the chart will taper off to both sides from this center value. Deviations from this pattern signal an anomaly, which can be used in the problem-solving process, as will be explained.

The normal distribution is a somewhat special distribution for various reasons. It is symmetric; that is, the likelihood of a data point being larger than the expected value is the same as for a data point being smaller than the expected value. The histogram based on such a distribution looks like a bell, thus another term for this distribution is *bell-shaped*.

This distribution, and many others, can also be used in the improvement method called *statistical process control* (SPC). In SPC, past data about the process and its results are used to calculate control limits for the process. If data points fall outside these limits or form certain patterns of plots in a so-called run chart, the process is out of control and must be corrected. Unfortunately, SPC can hardly be termed a simple tool so it falls outside the scope of this book, but we encourage readers who find the concept interesting to look up the further sources listed in the Additional Resources section.

Problem Solving

Root Cause Analysis

Problem Understanding

Problem Cause Brainstorming

Problem Cause Data Collection

Problem Cause Data Analysis

Root Cause Identification

Root Cause Elimination

Solution Implementation

Tool Selection

Example Cases

Problem Solving

Root Cause
Analysis

Problem
Understanding

Problem Cause
Brainstorming

Problem Cause
Data Collection

**Problem Cause
Data Analysis**

Root Cause
Identification

Root Cause
Elimination

Solution
Implementation

Tool Selection

Example Cases

THE STEPS IN USING HISTOGRAMS

1. Count the number of data points *N*. (To produce a valid histogram, you should have at least 30 data points.)

2. Calculate the numerical distance *R* between the largest and smallest values in the data.

3. Depending on the value of *N*, divide *R* into a number of classes *C* that can be found in this table:

The number of data points *N*	The number of classes *C*
Less than 50	5 to 7
50 to 100	6 to 10
100 to 250	7 to 12
More than 250	10 to 20

4. Determine the width of each class *H*. This is calculated through the following formula:

$$H = \frac{R}{C}$$

The width should always have as many decimals as the data points.

5. Determine the lower and upper values for the individual classes by setting the smallest value of the data set as the lower value for the first class. Find the upper value for this class by adding the class width to the lower value. The higher value of one class in turn becomes the lower value of the next class. Remember that the lower value is always included in its class (that is, ≥ lower value), while the upper value belongs to the next class (that is, < upper value).

6. To simplify the construction of the histogram, insert the data into a check sheet.

7. Construct the histogram based on the check sheet. Mark the classes along the horizontal axis and the frequency along the vertical. Use vertical bars to indicate the distribution among classes.

INTERPRETING A HISTOGRAM

Histogram patterns to be aware of include:

- One peak shows the mean value for the process. If this peak is not centered, there is often a special cause for it, which could prove interesting to look into.

- Two clear peaks could stem from two different data sources such as two operators, two shifts, two vendors, and so on (see example below). This should be checked.

- A cut-off pattern that shows no signs of tapering off suggests that data points are being subjected to some selection process during or after collection.

- A comb-like pattern indicates that too many classes have been defined. Some classes are unable to capture data points, rendering the chart useless.

Problem Solving

Root Cause Analysis

Problem Understanding

Problem Cause Brainstorming

Problem Cause Data Collection

Problem Cause Data Analysis

Root Cause Identification

Root Cause Elimination

Solution Implementation

Tool Selection

Example Cases

An Example of the Use of a Histogram

A small-town newspaper used children and adolescents to deliver the paper to subscribers. Frequent complaints about late deliveries suddenly started to occur on one particular paper route. When the carrier was confronted with the complaints, he was surprised, had no good explanation for the delays, but promised to keep up to standards. After a brief period of significantly reduced complaints, they picked up again to the old level. The distribution manager asked a sample of subscribers on the route to make a note of every time the paper was delayed, and by how much. After four weeks of registration, the distribution manager analyzed the data. (The resulting histogram is shown below.) When the paperboy was confronted with this, he confessed that on Mondays, Fridays, and Saturdays, his sister did the route for him. Being less familiar with the route and cycling slower, this caused delays on the average of 20 minutes.

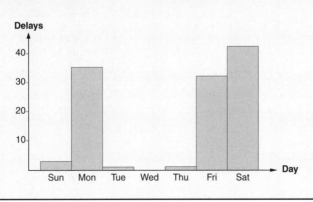

Problem Solving

Root Cause
Analysis

Problem
Understanding

Problem Cause
Brainstorming

Problem Cause
Data Collection

**Problem Cause
Data Analysis**

Root Cause
Identification

Root Cause
Elimination

Solution
Implementation

Tool Selection

Example Cases

CHECKLIST FOR HISTOGRAMS

❑ Collect and record the data for which the histogram will be produced.

❑ There should be at least 30 data points in the data set, thus making it valid for use with a histogram.

❑ Calculate the numerical distance between the largest and smallest values in the data set.

❑ Use the help table on page 88 to determine the number of classes in the histogram.

❑ Calculate the width of each class using the given formula.

❑ Determine the lower and upper values of each class, defining the border between them.

❑ Construct the histogram based on the defined classes and the collected data.

❑ Examine the resulting histogram to find any patterns. Analyze those patterns in terms of their causes.

HISTOGRAM TEMPLATE

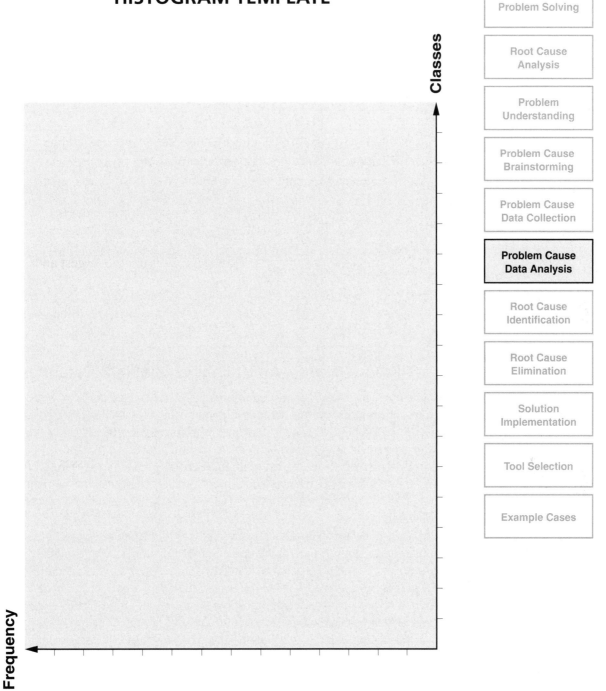

Classes

Frequency

Problem Solving

Root Cause
Analysis

Problem
Understanding

Problem Cause
Brainstorming

Problem Cause
Data Collection

**Problem Cause
Data Analysis**

Root Cause
Identification

Root Cause
Elimination

Solution
Implementation

Tool Selection

Example Cases

Problem Solving

Root Cause
Analysis

Problem
Understanding

Problem Cause
Brainstorming

Problem Cause
Data Collection

**Problem Cause
Data Analysis**

Root Cause
Identification

Root Cause
Elimination

Solution
Implementation

Tool Selection

Example Cases

THE PURPOSE AND APPLICATIONS OF PARETO CHARTS

The Pareto principle states that most effects, often 80 percent, are the result of a small number of causes, often only 20 percent. A healthy approach to root cause analysis is, therefore, to attack these 20 percent, often labeled "the vital few."

The main purpose of the Pareto chart is to display graphically this skewed distribution. The chart shows the causes of a problem sorted by their degree of seriousness, expressed as frequency of occurrence, costs, performance level, and so on.

In root cause analysis, the Pareto chart can be used to:

- Obtain a clearer picture of the set of causes by viewing them according to importance.

- Understand which causes need further investigation.

Vilfredo Pareto—An Unknown Quality Forerunner

If you are schooled in quality management, you have most certainly been told many great stories about famous quality gurus like Deming, Feigenbaum, Juran, and others. However, the man who formulated the Pareto principle was probably the first scientist to influence the quality movement.

Vilfredo Pareto, an Italian mathematician, formulated his Pareto principle during the 1800s. He was concerned with the distribution of the riches in society and claimed that 20 percent of the population owned 80 percent of the wealth.

Translated to modern quality terminology, the Pareto principle states that most effects are produced by a small number of causes. For example, usually 80 percent of the problems related to purchased materials are caused by 20 percent of the suppliers. More importantly, 80 percent of the costs connected to poor quality or generally low performance are caused by 20 percent of all possible causes.

When embarking on a problem-solving effort, start by attacking these 20 percent, which are often labeled "the vital few." This does not imply that the remaining 80 percent, the "important many," should be ignored. The Pareto principle simply suggests the order in which problems should be attacked.

THE STEPS IN USING PARETO CHARTS

1. Define the problem to be analyzed and the different potential causes that have been identified.

2. Decide which criterion to use when comparing the possible causes, normally issues such as how often the different causes occur, their consequences, or costs.

3. Define the time interval during which data will be collected and carry out the data collection for the selected criterion. Often, this task will already have been performed.

4. Place the causes from left to right on the horizontal axis of the chart, in descending relative importance. Draw rectangles to heights that represent this importance.

5. Mark the data value on the left vertical axis and the percentage value on the right, and draw a curve of cumulative importance along the top edges of the rectangles.

| Problem Solving |
| Root Cause Analysis |
| Problem Understanding |
| Problem Cause Brainstorming |
| Problem Cause Data Collection |
| **Problem Cause Data Analysis** |
| Root Cause Identification |
| Root Cause Elimination |
| Solution Implementation |
| Tool Selection |
| Example Cases |

An Example of the Use of a Pareto Chart

Many studios around the world make television commercials. One studio specialized in shooting ads starring cats. This proved very popular and the company prospered.

Lately, many of the shootings were taking much longer than planned, causing production delays despite the use of overtime and weekend shoots. These delays were related to several factors including, among others, lack of equipment, technical problems with audio and video, rework of scripts, and misbehaving cats.

In fact, this last issue seemed to be the dominant problem area, and it was decided to map over the next few weeks what seemed to cause the unrest. The set assistant on duty was to record what he or she believed to be the reason the cats caused problems. This was done dutifully, and after five weeks, during which the problem persisted, quite a few pages of notes had been filled. Some of the data are shown on the top of the next page.

Not knowing exactly how to attack this data, someone recommended using a Pareto chart to see what seemed to be the prevailing causes. The chart, shown on the bottom of the next page, led to changes related to the scheduling of shootings and the preparation of the cats.

PARETO CHART EXAMPLE—CAT STUDIO

Cause of cat distress	Time lost due to the cause (minutes)	Total time lost due to the cause (minutes)
Not been fed	4, 3, 5, 2, 5, 3	22
Not been cuddled	3, 3, 5, 3	14
Studio too cold	9, 2, 4, 6, 4, 5	30
Too much noise	20, 15, 35, 20, 9, 16	115
Smell of previous cat still present	41, 68, 39, 60, 29, 52, 19, 8	316
Surface to sit/lie on not appealing	2, 4, 1	7

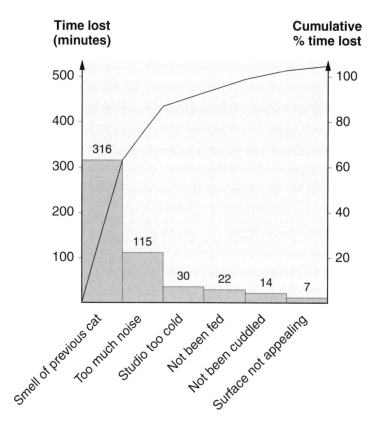

CHECKLIST FOR PARETO CHARTS

❑ Since use of the Pareto chart depends on a fixed set of causes, the problem and its probable causes must be defined first.

❑ Agree on which criterion will be used when ranking the possible causes.

❑ Set a time interval for collecting data about the causes and the defined criterion.

❑ Collect the data necessary to construct the chart, if you have not done so already.

❑ Draw the chart, placing the causes along the horizontal axis, the ranking criterion on the left vertical axis, and the cumulative criterion percentage on the right vertical axis.

❑ Rank the causes on the chart from left to right in descending order of importance according to the defined criterion.

❑ Draw rectangular bars on the chart. Heights should correspond with the importance of each cause.

❑ Insert the individual data values for each cause rectangle into the chart, on top of the rectangles.

❑ Draw a line indicating the cumulative importance along the top edges of the rectangles.

Problem Solving

Root Cause Analysis

Problem Understanding

Problem Cause Brainstorming

Problem Cause Data Collection

Problem Cause Data Analysis

Root Cause Identification

Root Cause Elimination

Solution Implementation

Tool Selection

Example Cases

Problem Solving

Root Cause
Analysis

Problem
Understanding

Problem Cause
Brainstorming

Problem Cause
Data Collection

**Problem Cause
Data Analysis**

Root Cause
Identification

Root Cause
Elimination

Solution
Implementation

Tool Selection

Example Cases

PARETO CHART TEMPLATE

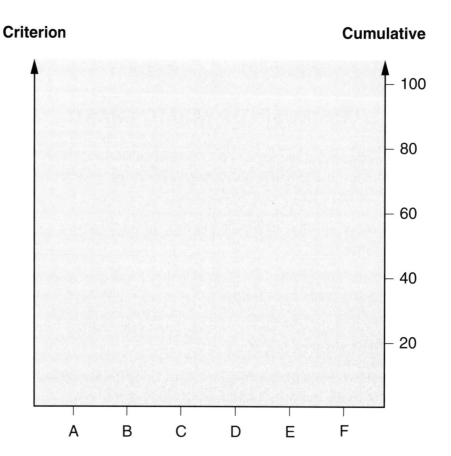

THE PURPOSE AND APPLICATIONS OF SCATTER CHARTS

Causes at different levels frequently impact one another. A scatter chart can identify such links between causes. (A prerequisite is that each cause can be expressed by a numerical value.)

The main purpose of the scatter chart is to show the relationship between two causes or other variables.

In root cause analysis, scatter charts are useful for:

- Exploring the chain of causes by understanding the impact one cause at one level has on the cause(s) at the next level

- Ruling out causes at different levels that are not linked to the root cause

| Problem Solving |
| Root Cause Analysis |
| Problem Understanding |
| Problem Cause Brainstorming |
| Problem Cause Data Collection |
| **Problem Cause Data Analysis** |
| Root Cause Identification |
| Root Cause Elimination |
| Solution Implementation |
| Tool Selection |
| Example Cases |

Types of Correlation

A two-dimensional scatter chart can analyze only two causes, expressed by a suitable variable, at the same time. When one of the variables increases, the other can also increase, decrease, or display random variation. If the two variables seem to change in synchronization, it might indicate that they are related to and impact each other.

The correlation between the variables being examined can range from highly positive to highly negative. Between these two extremes, there are weaker degrees of both positive and negative correlation, as well as no correlation. Examples of different scatter charts for different degrees of correlation are shown below.

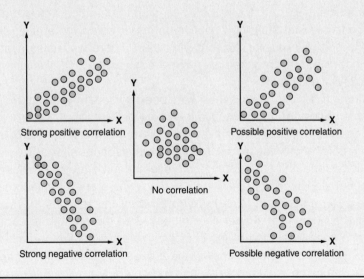

THE STEPS IN USING SCATTER CHARTS

1. Select the two variables (one independent and one dependent) to be examined.

2. For each value of the independent variable, measure the corresponding value of the dependent variable.

3. These two values form a data pair to be plotted on the chart. Typically, there should be at least 30, but preferably more than 100, data pairs to produce a meaningful chart.

4. Draw the chart by placing the independent, or expected cause, variable on the horizontal axis, and the dependent, or expected effect, variable on the vertical axis.

5. Plot and analyze the collected data pairs in the chart.

6. If the chart shows no correlation, plot the data pairs in a logarithmic chart, which can sometimes reveal connections not visible in a chart with ordinary axes.

An Example of the Use of a Scatter Chart

A large aluminumworks company ran five shifts all year long, with the shifts divided into teams manning one furnace each. A new pay system was introduced whereby the teams were continuously measured on their output, energy use, defect rate, and scrap metal use. The pay for the entire team, in turn, was linked to their performance in these categories.

The pay system was well liked, but now and then there were complaints that when shifts started, the first shift filled up the furnace with scrap metal. This made the first shift look good in terms of scrap metal use, but lowered the output levels for the following team. There were also complaints about poor cleaning, required maintenance not performed, vehicles parked haphazardly, and so on.

Although all of these issues had been raised by management, the problems persisted irregularly. Management believed that the pay system, although having raised productivity by close to two percent, was the cause of the trouble, and it was terminated in the early spring. After a few weeks of operations under the old system, there seemed to be more complaints than ever about sloppiness of personnel when leaving a shift. Baffled, the management ran a series of tests to try to pinpoint the reasons for this. They designed a number of scatter charts that linked the number of complaints with various causes. One of the charts revealed the culprit; as the scatter chart on the following page shows, there seemed to be a clear correlation between the number of complaints and the weather, apparently because the shift teams wanted to get off work and out into good weather as soon as possible, thus not cleaning up properly after themselves.

SCATTER CHART EXAMPLE— ALUMINUMWORKS

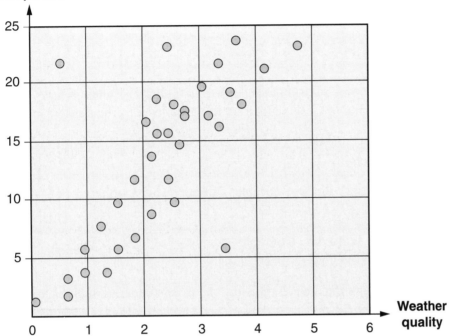

Problem Solving

Root Cause Analysis

Problem Understanding

Problem Cause Brainstorming

Problem Cause Data Collection

Problem Cause Data Analysis

Root Cause Identification

Root Cause Elimination

Solution Implementation

Tool Selection

Example Cases

A Word of Warning on Correlation

Two variables changing in a pattern of covariance might be correlated, which is an important finding. However, please keep in mind that even if there is some degree of synchronized variation between variables, it does not mean for certain that there is a cause-and-effect relationship between them. Indeed, a third variable may be causing the effects.

An astonishing example of an obvious miscorrelation was a scatter chart that showed a perfect covariation between the Dow Jones index and the water level of Lake Superior from 1925 to 1965.

Thus, if a scatter chart shows signs of correlation, investigate further for confirmation. Correspondingly, a chart that indicates no correlation should not lead you to dismiss your suspicions.

Problem Solving

Root Cause
Analysis

Problem
Understanding

Problem Cause
Brainstorming

Problem Cause
Data Collection

**Problem Cause
Data Analysis**

Root Cause
Identification

Root Cause
Elimination

Solution
Implementation

Tool Selection

Example Cases

CHECKLIST FOR SCATTER CHARTS

❑ If there is a larger experiment involving a number of correlation tests, the entire set of variables must be defined.

❑ Select and define the two variables to be analyzed in the chart.

❑ Measure the two variables, if data has not already been collected.

❑ The set of data pairs must consist of at least 30, but preferably more than 100 pairs.

❑ Design the chart by placing the independent variable on the horizontal axis. The independent variable is the factor believed to be governing the relationship between the two variables.

❑ On the vertical axis, place the dependent variable—that is, the factor believed to change in proportion to the independent variable.

❑ Plot the data pairs on the chart.

❑ Examine the completed chart, looking for patterns that indicate a connection between the two variables.

❑ If no such patterns emerge, draw the chart over again using logarithmic scales on one or both axes, as this "condenses" the plot and can make otherwise difficult-to-see patterns visible.

❑ If correlation patterns are identified, investigate any third variable involvement before drawing definite conclusions.

SCATTER CHART TEMPLATE

Dependent variable

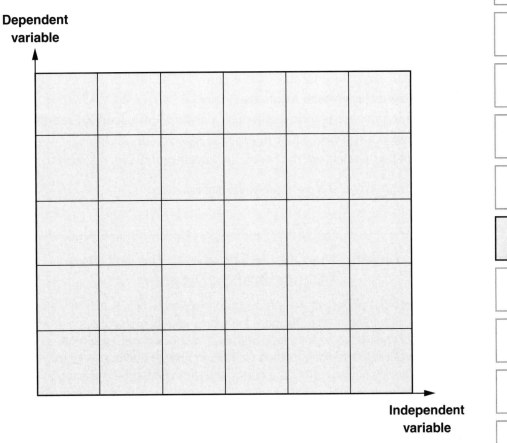

Independent variable

Problem Solving

Root Cause Analysis

Problem Understanding

Problem Cause Brainstorming

Problem Cause Data Collection

Problem Cause Data Analysis

Root Cause Identification

Root Cause Elimination

Solution Implementation

Tool Selection

Example Cases

Problem Solving

Root Cause
Analysis

Problem
Understanding

Problem Cause
Brainstorming

Problem Cause
Data Collection

**Problem Cause
Data Analysis**

Root Cause
Identification

Root Cause
Elimination

Solution
Implementation

Tool Selection

Example Cases

THE PURPOSE AND APPLICATIONS OF PROBLEM CONCENTRATION DIAGRAMS

The check sheet presented in the previous chapter is a practical tool to use when collecting data about a problem. When analyzing these, or other data, afterward, a problem concentration diagram is helpful in connecting registered problems to physical locations.

Its main purpose is to reveal patterns of problem occurrence, especially in cases where problems occur in physical systems or facilities.

In root cause analysis, the problem concentration chart is used to:

• Identify any patterns in problem occurrences.

Linking the Check Sheet with the Problem Concentration Diagram

As mentioned above, there is a clear connection between these two tools. The check sheet is used to record when or where problems occur over a period of time. Upon examination of a filled-in check sheet, simply identifying concentrations of registrations can lead to important findings.

However, equally often, the check sheet data must be analyzed further to produce additional insight. Especially in situations where problems occur at different places in a product, facility, or other type of physical system, using a problem concentration diagram to further the analysis often produces good results.

The problem concentration diagram can also be used directly as both a data registration tool and analysis tool. In this case, the data are registered directly onto the diagram without going through the step of using check sheets.

THE STEPS IN USING PROBLEM CONCENTRATION DIAGRAMS

1. Determine whether suitable problem occurrence data already exist; if yes, skip to step 4.

2. If not, clearly define what events are to be recorded and assign a symbol to each type of problem or event.

3. Define the period for data recording and suitable intervals.

4. Design the diagram by drawing a map of the system, object, or area.

5. Populate the diagram with problem registration data, either using existing data or through recording problem occurrences directly onto the diagram.

6. Analyze the diagram to identify patterns of problem occurrences.

An Example of the Use of a Problem Concentration Diagram

A large clothing store saw losses due to steadily increasing theft, despite attaching alarms to about half of the garments displayed. All types of clothes were stocked, but there were obvious differences among the types of garments stolen. Using a check sheet to record the types of clothes that were stolen during a period of one month confirmed this. However, when looking more closely at the types of garments most often stolen, none of the store staff understood why these particular types were so popular among dishonest customers.

After catching a thief red-handed one day trying to put a sweater into a shopping bag from another store, one of the employees realized that the particular section of the store was vulnerable. It was hidden from easy view of the checkout counter and could not be observed using security cameras either.

Having data available already from the check sheet registrations, the store constructed a problem concentration diagram for the store. A map was drawn of the store facility, and the garments stolen were depicted on the map. It quickly became obvious that almost all the items stolen were from areas with the same type of vulnerability.

The alarm procedure was changed, and alarms consistently attached to all items displayed in such areas. Although thieves still take garments from these areas by tearing off the alarms, the problem has been significantly reduced.

Problem Solving

Root Cause Analysis

Problem Understanding

Problem Cause Brainstorming

Problem Cause Data Collection

Problem Cause Data Analysis

Root Cause Identification

Root Cause Elimination

Solution Implementation

Tool Selection

Example Cases

PROBLEM CONCENTRATION DIAGRAM
EXAMPLE—CLOTHING STORE

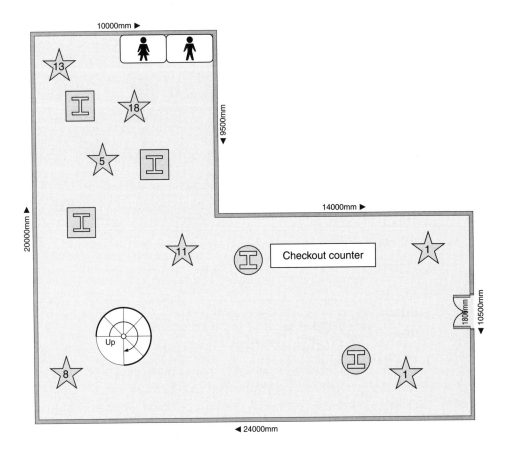

CHECKLIST FOR PROBLEM CONCENTRATION DIAGRAMS

❑ Determine whether suitable problem occurrence data already exist that can be used to construct the diagram. If so, this will obviously make the job easier.

❑ If not, the procedure outlined for check sheets should be followed, deciding on the collection period and dividing it into suitable intervals.

❑ Define the problem events to be recorded, and, if different types of problems are expected to occur, decide on a unique symbol for each to use in the diagram.

❑ Design the diagram by drawing a map of the system, object, or area, using illustrations where possible as this makes for a more realistic diagram. Especially in the case of several people registering data, the more realistic the map, the easier it is to make accurate registrations.

❑ If a data set is not already available, collect data during the entire collection period, emphasizing accurate registration.

❑ Populate the map by plotting the occurrences, using the designated symbols or numbers to represent concentration, on the diagram.

❑ Identify the most frequently occurring events and examine where these occur.

❑ Look for the reasons behind the pattern to discover the most important problem causes.

Problem Solving

Root Cause Analysis

Problem Understanding

Problem Cause Brainstorming

Problem Cause Data Collection

Problem Cause Data Analysis

Root Cause Identification

Root Cause Elimination

Solution Implementation

Tool Selection

Example Cases

Problem Solving

Root Cause
Analysis

Problem
Understanding

Problem Cause
Brainstorming

Problem Cause
Data Collection

**Problem Cause
Data Analysis**

Root Cause
Identification

Root Cause
Elimination

Solution
Implementation

Tool Selection

Example Cases

THE PURPOSE AND APPLICATIONS
OF RELATIONS DIAGRAMS

A relations diagram borders on being a tool for root cause identification but is mainly used to identify logical relationships in a complex and confusing problem situation. In such cases, the strength of a relations diagram is its ability to visualize such relationships.

A relations diagram's main purpose is to help identify relationships that are not easily recognizable.

In root cause analysis, this is particularly useful for:

• Understanding how different aspects of the problem are connected

• Seeing relationships between the problem and its possible causes that can be further analyzed

Two Types of Relations Diagrams

There are two types of relations diagrams:

• Qualitative relations diagrams

• Quantitative relations diagrams

Both diagrams are based on the principle of identifying relationships among different factors, but they differ in their approach. In the qualitative version, the factors to be analyzed are simply plotted on an empty chart and relationships are found by connecting the factors based on an intuitive understanding of them. Thus, this variant can produce unreliable results.

In the quantitative type, a simpler numerical approach is used to determine the relationships between different factors. Since this approach is more structured, it is usually easier to drive this process toward a completed analysis. For these reasons, the quantitative relations diagram is the one presented in this book.

THE STEPS IN USING RELATIONS DIAGRAMS

1. Determine the factors to be analyzed for possible relationships and label these using brief and succinct definitions.

2. Plot the factors on an empty chart on a whiteboard, preferably in a roughly circular shape.

3. Assess what impacts each factor and which factors are impacted by it, and illustrate the relationships using arrows.

4. After all relationships have been assessed, count the number of arrows pointing into and away from each factor and denote this information on the diagram.

5. Depending on the number of arrows pointing in each direction for a factor, it can play one of two roles: driver (more arrows away from than into), or indicator (more arrows into than away from).

6. When continuing the root cause analysis, the drivers form the starting point.

An Example of the Use of a Relations Diagram

A small hospital was concerned about the productivity of its doctors, as they were the most expensive employees and were critical for the treatment of the patients. Having taken numerous steps toward ensuring high productivity, hospital management was baffled when productivity steadily declined month after month.

Since this disturbing development was unexplainable, management decided to gain some insight into causes and effects among the different factors at play. A relations diagram was seen as an ideal vehicle for this, and the following factors were included in the analysis:

- The number of scheduled appointments per doctor
- The number of emergency appointments per doctor
- Administrative workload per doctor
- The number of changes in scheduled appointments
- Equipment quality and reliability
- Nurse availability
- Availability of other support functions
- The pay level of doctors

When the relations diagram shown on the following page had been completed, attention shifted from improving the doctors' work situation to ensuring the availability of nurses, other support functions, and operational equipment.

Problem Solving

Root Cause Analysis

Problem Understanding

Problem Cause Brainstorming

Problem Cause Data Collection

Problem Cause Data Analysis

Root Cause Identification

Root Cause Elimination

Solution Implementation

Tool Selection

Example Cases

RELATIONS DIAGRAM EXAMPLE—HOSPITAL

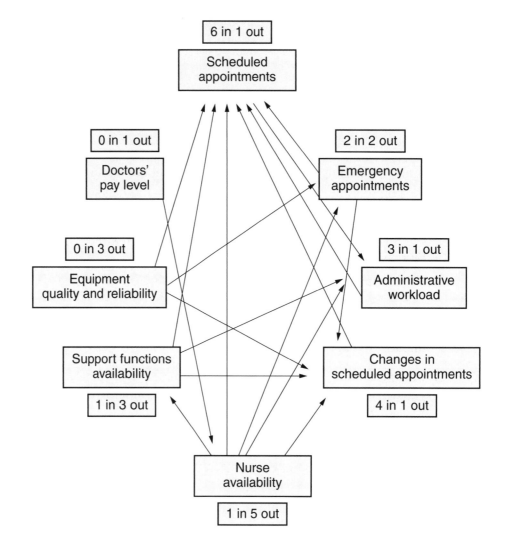

CHECKLIST FOR RELATIONS DIAGRAMS

❑ Determine the factors you want included in the analysis for possible relationships.

❑ Label these factors using brief and succinct definitions.

❑ Plot the factors, identified by their labels, in small boxes on an empty chart on a whiteboard, preferably in a roughly circular shape.

❑ For each factor in the analysis, assess what factors impact it and are impacted by it.

❑ Illustrate the impacts using arrows between the factors, pointing from the impacting factor to the one being impacted.

❑ Count the number of arrows pointing toward and away from each factor and write this information on the chart next to the factor.

❑ Divide the factors into drivers and indicators based on whether more impact arrows point away or toward them.

❑ Later in the analysis, use the drivers as starting points for identifying the causes of the problem.

Problem Solving

Root Cause Analysis

Problem Understanding

Problem Cause Brainstorming

Problem Cause Data Collection

Problem Cause Data Analysis

Root Cause Identification

Root Cause Elimination

Solution Implementation

Tool Selection

Example Cases

Problem Solving

Root Cause
Analysis

Problem
Understanding

Problem Cause
Brainstorming

Problem Cause
Data Collection

**Problem Cause
Data Analysis**

Root Cause
Identification

Root Cause
Elimination

Solution
Implementation

Tool Selection

Example Cases

RELATIONS DIAGRAM TEMPLATE

in   out

in   out

in   out

in   out

in   out

in   out

THE PURPOSE AND APPLICATIONS OF AFFINITY DIAGRAMS

The previously presented problem cause data analysis tools are mostly applicable when the data are in a numerical form. To analyze qualitative data, an affinity diagram is useful. It groups data and finds underlying relationships connecting the resulting groups.

This tool allows the user to see relationships between seemingly unrelated ideas, conditions, or meanings.

In root cause analysis, some uses of affinity diagrams include:

- Exploring relationships between different causes, often at different levels in the cause hierarchy

- Grouping related causes into classes that might be treated collectively later on in the analysis

---

The Origins of the Affinity Diagram

While most of the root cause analysis tools stem from precise scientific fields like mathematics, statistics, and so on, the affinity diagram was invented in a field far from these.

The tool is known by several names. In addition to affinity diagram or chart, it is also called a KJ chart, so named for Jiro Kawakita, a Japanese anthropologist who invented the KJ method, a precursor to the KJ chart.

This also has some implications for the use of the tool. While many tools require a precise mind geared toward accuracy, the affinity diagram is typically a creative technique that requires an open mind on the part of participants.

Problem Solving

Root Cause Analysis

Problem Understanding

Problem Cause Brainstorming

Problem Cause Data Collection

Problem Cause Data Analysis

Root Cause Identification

Root Cause Elimination

Solution Implementation

Tool Selection

Example Cases

Problem Solving

Root Cause
Analysis

Problem
Understanding

Problem Cause
Brainstorming

Problem Cause
Data Collection

**Problem Cause
Data Analysis**

Root Cause
Identification

Root Cause
Elimination

Solution
Implementation

Tool Selection

Example Cases

THE STEPS IN USING AFFINITY DIAGRAMS

1. Gather the participants in a room that has a large whiteboard. Write the topic to be analyzed in large letters at the top of the board, preferably in neutral terms, and underlined.

2. Take possible causes from the previous stage, or brainstorm them, and write these causes on adhesive notes. These should be succinctly formulated but never as only one single word. Attach the notes to the board in a totally random pattern.

3. In silence, without any discussion, the group moves the notes around, trying to form groups of causes that are related. Usually the notes are moved many times before they find their places. Depending on the number of ideas, this might easily take an hour or more.

4. After grouping ideas, the participants discuss the final shape of the chart. As the motives for placing notes in specific spots are explained, minor movements should be allowed. The total number of groups should not exceed five to ten.

5. Create titles for the groups, dividing larger groups into subgroups at lower levels.

6. Finalize the chart by drawing boxes around the groups and possibly adding arrows between them to indicate additional relationships.

7. Evaluate the chart with regard to further efforts. The groups contain elements and suggestions of causes that affect one another and, thus, must be seen in connection when devising solutions.

AFFINITY DIAGRAM EXAMPLE— FURNITURE MANUFACTURER

Possible causes for delays in the assembly process

Wooden parts	Metal parts	Tools++	Operators	Environment
Inaccurate wooden parts dimensions	Wrong sets of screws	Tools not available	Operator poorly trained	Temperature too high
Bent wooden parts	Damaged threads	Out of glue	Transport out of assembly shop too slow	Humidity too high
Late-arriving wooden parts	Broken handles	Defective jigs		Too much noise to concentrate properly
Wooden parts with surface imperfections	Late-arriving metal parts	Broken tools		
		Incorrect assembly step must be redone		

Problem Solving

Root Cause Analysis

Problem Understanding

Problem Cause Brainstorming

Problem Cause Data Collection

Problem Cause Data Analysis

Root Cause Identification

Root Cause Elimination

Solution Implementation

Tool Selection

Example Cases

An Example of the Use of an Affinity Diagram

A furniture manufacturer delivered, among many other products, a line of chests of drawers. The assembly of these generally took much longer than the calculated assembly time, on which all production plans and delivery schedules were based. From a brief evaluation of the situation, it was clear that there were many different reasons why the assembly process took so long.

Some of the assembly workers and employees from departments supplying parts and services to them teamed up to look into these causes in more detail. They realized that many of the identified reasons were related—some directly, others more loosely. To better understand these relationships, the employees made an affinity diagram to help clarify the situation.

The resulting diagram, shown above, emerged from a run-through of the main steps in the process for designing such a chart. The groups of probable causes represented a good starting point for determining which categories caused the most harm.

Problem Solving

Root Cause
Analysis

Problem
Understanding

Problem Cause
Brainstorming

Problem Cause
Data Collection

**Problem Cause
Data Analysis**

Root Cause
Identification

Root Cause
Elimination

Solution
Implementation

Tool Selection

Example Cases

CHECKLIST FOR AFFINITY DIAGRAMS

❑ Find a suitable room for the exercise, containing a large whiteboard and adhesive notes.

❑ Write the topic—that is, a problem or its causes—near the top of the whiteboard.

❑ Either analyze causes of the problem that were gathered in the possible cause brainstorming stage or brainstorm them now.

❑ Write the possible causes on the adhesive notes, in neutral terms, and attach them to the whiteboard in a random pattern.

❑ Hold a session where the participants silently move the causes around to group them.

❑ Discuss the groupings and possible adjustments allowed, arriving at no more than five to ten groups of causes.

❑ Create titles for each of the groups.

❑ Draw boxes around the groups and add arrows to symbolize additional relationships to complete the chart.

❑ Decide on a further course of action concerning the groups of possible causes and their treatment.

PROBLEM CAUSE DATA ANALYSIS CHECKLIST

Although root cause analysis is not one clear process from start to finish, some distinct stages in the analysis are discernible. This checklist should help assess whether the most important elements of the problem cause data analysis stage have been accomplished before moving on.

❏ Use one or more data sets pertaining to the problem at hand and its possible causes as the starting point of the problem cause data analysis stage.

❏ Assess the collected data and desired analysis to determine which tool to use. Consider whether one-dimensional effects are likely to be found, if correlation between two or more groups of data is expected, if location differences are likely, the complexity of the data, and so on.

❏ Choose among the following analysis tools: histograms, Pareto charts, scatter charts, problem concentration diagrams, relations diagrams, and affinity diagrams.

❏ Conduct the analysis according to the steps of the selected tool or tools.

❏ If more than one tool is applied, compare the conclusions from each analysis for opposing or matching results.

❏ Carry the conclusions from the problem cause data analysis stage forward into the root cause identification stage.

Problem Solving

Root Cause Analysis

Problem Understanding

Problem Cause Brainstorming

Problem Cause Data Collection

Problem Cause Data Analysis

Root Cause Identification

Root Cause Elimination

Solution Implementation

Tool Selection

Example Cases

7

Tools for Root Cause Identification

Problem Solving

Root Cause
Analysis

Problem
Understanding

Problem Cause
Brainstorming

Problem Cause
Data Collection

Problem Cause
Data Analysis

**Root Cause
Identification**

Root Cause
Elimination

Solution
Implementation

Tool Selection

Example Cases

This chapter presents four individual tools and techniques for the purpose of identifying the root cause of the problem studied. Other tools are available as well, but they are considerably more complex and often require advanced calculations. Such tools have been eliminated from our discussion, so we can keep the approaches simple and straightforward to apply.

Problem Solving
Root Cause Analysis
Problem Understanding
Problem Cause Brainstorming
Problem Cause Data Collection
Problem Cause Data Analysis
Root Cause Identification
Root Cause Elimination
Solution Implementation
Tool Selection
Example Cases

ROOT CAUSE IDENTIFICATION

You are finally here! From the list of possible causes you have created and analyzed during the four previous stages, you are now ready to identify the culprit, the root cause.

In terms of duration and complexity, this stage is rarely the most difficult or longest-lasting. With thorough preparation, you can normally proceed through this stage quickly.

The tools available for the identification process are:

- Cause-and-effect chart

- Matrix diagram

- Five whys

- Fault tree analysis

Finding the Root Cause Can Require Several Iterations

It has been mentioned several times already throughout the book, but it warrants repeating: although the chapters of this book and the tools associated with each of them can give the impression that root cause analysis is simple and straightforward, this is certainly not always true.

In many cases, tools and techniques have to be used several times to enable drilling down to the real root cause. Tools can be successfully applied in quite different phases than where they have been presented in this book, and the order of the phases can often be changed.

This is quite normal, so please keep in mind that the placement of the tools and the applications described here are only indications of the most typical cases. Feel completely free to experiment by using them elsewhere and for different purposes.

THE PURPOSE AND APPLICATIONS OF CAUSE-AND-EFFECT CHARTS

The name of the cause-and-effect chart tool defines what it is about: a chart that analyzes relationships between a problem and its causes. It combines aspects of brainstorming with systematic analysis to create a powerful technique. The tool is also known as an Ishikawa diagram, named for its inventor.

In the larger framework of root cause analysis, this tool's main purpose is to understand what causes a problem. It can be used to:

- Generate and group problem causes.

- Systematically evaluate the causes and determine which are most likely to be root causes.

Two Types of Cause-and-Effect Charts

The cause-and-effect chart has so far been described as if it were one singular chart, but there are at least two types of cause-and-effect charts:

- *Fishbone chart.* The traditional method of constructing such charts, where the main product is a chart whose shape resembles a fishbone.

- *Process chart.* More directly focused on the analysis of problems inside business processes. For each step of the process that is believed to create problems, a fishbone chart is constructed to address all potential causes of less-than-expected performance. After individual charts are designed, a collective analysis is conducted to identify the causes of highest importance.

The traditional fishbone chart type is discussed here, including two distinctly different ways of creating the chart.

- *Dispersion analysis.* The problem being analyzed is drawn on the right-hand side of the chart, at the end of a large arrow. Main groups of probable causes are drawn as branches to the arrow. For each branch, all possible causes are identified.

- *Cause enumeration.* All probable causes are brainstormed and listed in the order they are generated. The causes are then grouped into main categories and written on the fishbone chart.

The end product is the same regardless of the approach used. Our focus here is dispersion analysis.

Problem Solving

Root Cause Analysis

Problem Understanding

Problem Cause Brainstorming

Problem Cause Data Collection

Problem Cause Data Analysis

Root Cause Identification

Root Cause Elimination

Solution Implementation

Tool Selection

Example Cases

Problem Solving

Root Cause
Analysis

Problem
Understanding

Problem Cause
Brainstorming

Problem Cause
Data Collection

Problem Cause
Data Analysis

**Root Cause
Identification**

Root Cause
Elimination

Solution
Implementation

Tool Selection

Example Cases

THE STEPS IN USING CAUSE-AND-EFFECT CHARTS

1. Clearly describe the problem for which causes are sought.

2. Using a whiteboard or some other large surface, draw the problem at the right end of a large arrow. Allow space for the causes to be generated. Do not strive for symmetry and graphic effects.

3. Identify the main categories of causes of the problem and write them on branches emanating from the large arrow.

4. Brainstorm and write all possible causes in the applicable area(s) of the chart. Use brief and succinct descriptions. Proceed through the chart one main category at a time. Write causes that belong under more than one category in all relevant positions.

5. Analyze the identified causes to determine the most likely root causes.

An Example of the Use of a Cause-and-Effect Chart

A company operating cable television services had seen consistently high employee absenteeism, especially in the installation and service department. Besides costing the company a lot of money, this absenteeism angered many customers, because hook-ups were not done at the scheduled time and problems took unacceptably long to correct.

Among other steps taken to improve the situation, the human resource manager and some service personnel turned to different problem-solving tools. First they conducted a brainstorming session that generated many ideas as to why absenteeism was so high, then analyzed these ideas using a cause-and-effect chart.

The brainstorming session generated many ideas, some more creative, and perhaps less realistic, than others. After sorting the ideas and picking those most likely to be relevant and curable causes, the group analyzed and grouped the causes on the chart. The resulting diagram is shown on the following page. The results led the company to consider training programs, reward systems, and increasing the quality of the tools and equipment used by the service personnel.

CAUSE-AND-EFFECT CHART EXAMPLE—CABLE TELEVISION COMPANY

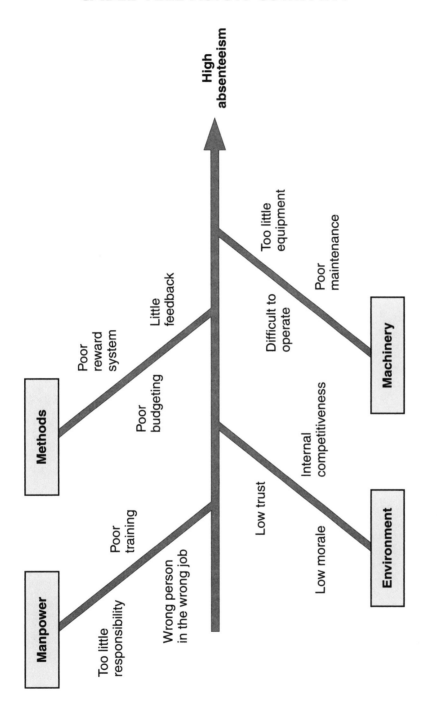

Problem Solving

Root Cause Analysis

Problem Understanding

Problem Cause Brainstorming

Problem Cause Data Collection

Problem Cause Data Analysis

Root Cause Identification

Root Cause Elimination

Solution Implementation

Tool Selection

Example Cases

Problem Solving

Root Cause
Analysis

Problem
Understanding

Problem Cause
Brainstorming

Problem Cause
Data Collection

Problem Cause
Data Analysis

**Root Cause
Identification**

Root Cause
Elimination

Solution
Implementation

Tool Selection

Example Cases

CHECKLIST FOR
CAUSE-AND-EFFECT CHARTS

❏ Clearly define and describe the problem under analysis to allow a targeted analysis session.

❏ Write the problem at the end of a large arrow on a whiteboard or some other suitable surface.

❏ When drawing the chart, allow sufficient space to write many ideas and causes; don't worry about making your chart neat at this stage of the analysis.

❏ Define the main groups of causes and write them at the ends of "branches" pointing to the large arrow.

❏ Write possible causes of the problem along appropriate branches of the 'fishbone,' based either on a previously conducted brainstorming session or on brainstorming done while constructing the chart.

❏ Strive for brief and succinct descriptions when writing the causes on the chart.

❏ After assigning all causes to the appropriate branch(es), evaluate the different groups of causes one at a time.

❏ Identify the most important causes and pinpoint possible root causes.

CAUSE-AND-EFFECT CHART TEMPLATE

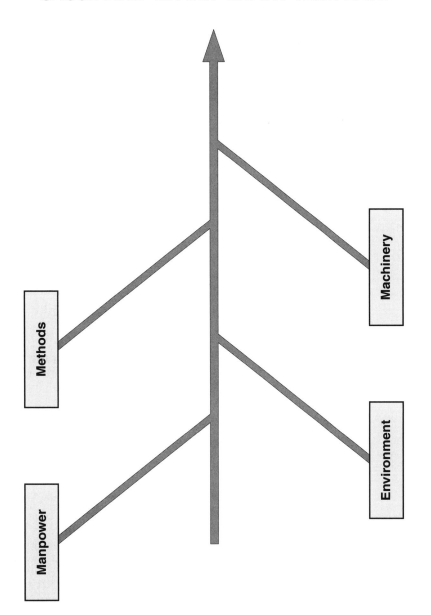

Methods

Manpower

Machinery

Environment

Problem Solving

Root Cause
Analysis

Problem
Understanding

Problem Cause
Brainstorming

Problem Cause
Data Collection

Problem Cause
Data Analysis

**Root Cause
Identification**

Root Cause
Elimination

Solution
Implementation

Tool Selection

Example Cases

Problem Solving

Root Cause
Analysis

Problem
Understanding

Problem Cause
Brainstorming

Problem Cause
Data Collection

Problem Cause
Data Analysis

**Root Cause
Identification**

Root Cause
Elimination

Solution
Implementation

Tool Selection

Example Cases

THE PURPOSE AND APPLICATIONS OF MATRIX DIAGRAMS

The second tool used at this stage of the root cause analysis allows you to investigate a number of possible causes and determine which contributes most to the problem being analyzed. The tool's strength lies in its ability to graphically portray multiple connections.

The main purpose of the matrix diagram is to analyze causal relationships between possible causes and problems.

In root cause analysis, this can be used for:

- Mapping the overall impact of different possible causes of the problem

- Determining which of many causes is the most prominent, thus usually the root cause

Several Types of Matrix Diagrams

Many different matrix diagrams can be used, depending on the number of variables studied. Some common ones are shown here.

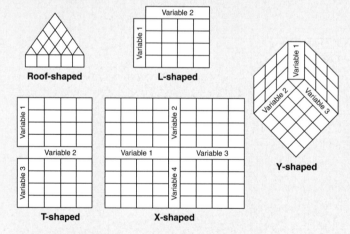

In root cause analysis, the most widely used type of diagram is the L-shaped matrix, which places the problem characteristics on one axis and the possible causes on the other. The other types of matrix diagrams are not described here.

THE STEPS IN USING MATRIX DIAGRAMS

1. Select the problem characteristics and possible causes to be analyzed for types and levels of relationships.

2. Create an empty matrix of suitable size.

3. Plot the variables on the diagram.

4. Indicate impacts by using the symbols shown below.

5. For each column in the diagram, calculate the total impact and present the sum.

6. Possible causes with a large sum are likely root causes.

Relation	Symbol	Weight
Weak	△	1
Medium	○	3
Strong	◉	9

An Example of the Use of a Matrix Diagram

A taxi operator in a large city had seen that competing for customers on streets, at airports, and so on, generated long periods of waiting time during which potential revenue was lost. It had therefore specialized in pre-order customers like hotels, hospitals, and private companies. This strategy had been successful, but lately the company had received many customer complaints related to tardy pick-up and delivery, poorly cleaned cars, discourteous drivers, and other less serious issues. Reliability, service, and their customers' ability to trust them were crucial for success, so this problem had to be solved.

It seemed to the administration, the dispatching central, and the drivers that the main cause for the delays was unpredictable traffic. Many other options had been mentioned as well, so a small improvement team used a matrix diagram to see if any of these other possible causes were important.

The resulting matrix diagram is shown on the following page. As you can see, when the larger situation had been carefully considered, there were at least four other factors that probably caused many of the problems. Putting measures in place to remedy these factors did produce improvement.

Problem Solving

Root Cause Analysis

Problem Understanding

Problem Cause Brainstorming

Problem Cause Data Collection

Problem Cause Data Analysis

Root Cause Identification

Root Cause Elimination

Solution Implementation

Tool Selection

Example Cases

Problem Solving

Root Cause Analysis

Problem Understanding

Problem Cause Brainstorming

Problem Cause Data Collection

Problem Cause Data Analysis

Root Cause Identification

Root Cause Elimination

Solution Implementation

Tool Selection

Example Cases

MATRIX DIAGRAM EXAMPLE— TAXI COMPANY

Problem characteristic	Unpredictable traffic	Late dispatch	Too many rides per car	Poor route planning	No car wash machine	Inaccurate address info	Old cars
Late pickup	●	●	○	●	◁	●	○
Late delivery	●	●	○	●			○
Dirty car exterior			●	◁	●		○
Dirty car interior			●		●		○
Rude driver	◁	○	○	◁		●	
Bumpy ride				○			
Baggage space							○
Total impact score	19	21	27	23	19	18	15

Possible causes

CHECKLIST FOR MATRIX DIAGRAMS

❑ Carefully select the problem characteristics and the possible causes of the problem, making sure not to exclude any possible causes from the analysis.

❑ Create an empty matrix diagram, leaving space for the selected number of problem characteristics and possible causes.

❑ Plot these variables on the matrix diagram.

❑ Assess each possible cause and its impact on each of the problem characteristics and place the appropriate impact symbol on the matrix.

❑ When all impact combinations have been evaluated, calculate the total impact scores for each possible cause by summing the corresponding impact factors for each of the impact symbols.

❑ Write the total impact scores on the matrix.

❑ Identify the possible causes with the largest total impact scores, as these are likely root causes of the problem.

Problem Solving

Root Cause Analysis

Problem Understanding

Problem Cause Brainstorming

Problem Cause Data Collection

Problem Cause Data Analysis

Root Cause Identification

Root Cause Elimination

Solution Implementation

Tool Selection

Example Cases

Problem Solving

Root Cause
Analysis

Problem
Understanding

Problem Cause
Brainstorming

Problem Cause
Data Collection

Problem Cause
Data Analysis

**Root Cause
Identification**

Root Cause
Elimination

Solution
Implementation

Tool Selection

Example Cases

MATRIX DIAGRAM TEMPLATE

Possible causes

Problem
characteristic

Total

THE PURPOSE AND APPLICATIONS OF FIVE WHYS

Five whys is also known as the *why–why chart* and *root cause analysis*. Its inherent nature is to delve ever more deeply into the levels of causes, thus resembling the wider concept of root cause analysis itself.

Its main purpose is to constantly ask "Why?" when a cause has been identified, thus progressing through the levels toward the root cause.

In a wider root cause analysis, five whys can be used to:

- Question whether each identified cause is a symptom, a lower-level cause, or a root cause.

- Continue the search for true root causes even after a possible cause has been found.

Stop the Questioning in Time

The key concept of the five whys technique is to keep posing the question "Why?" whenever a new cause has been identified. Each time the why question is answered by bringing up another cause at a higher level in the cause hierarchy, immediately ask again, "Why?" This relentless approach keeps those working on the problem on their toes, thus not allowing them to settle for anything less than the root cause.

However, there comes a point in the chain of causes where no further causes can possibly be found. This last cause is, as you know, the root cause—the point at which you should stop asking why. For those who are religious, it is possible to argue that there is another level, namely God, behind everything that happens. In root cause analysis, it is wise to stop before you reach this level, as it could prove very difficult to do anything about.

Problem Solving

Root Cause Analysis

Problem Understanding

Problem Cause Brainstorming

Problem Cause Data Collection

Problem Cause Data Analysis

Root Cause Identification

Root Cause Elimination

Solution Implementation

Tool Selection

Example Cases

Problem Solving

Root Cause
Analysis

Problem
Understanding

Problem Cause
Brainstorming

Problem Cause
Data Collection

Problem Cause
Data Analysis

**Root Cause
Identification**

Root Cause
Elimination

Solution
Implementation

Tool Selection

Example Cases

THE STEPS IN USING FIVE WHYS

1. Determine the starting point of the analysis, either a problem or an already identified cause that should be further analyzed.

2. Use brainstorming, brainwriting, and other approaches to find causes at the level below the starting point.

3. Ask "Why is this a cause of the original problem?" for each identified cause.

4. Depict the chain of causes as a sequence of text on a whiteboard.

5. For each new answer to the question, ask the question again, continuing until no new answer results. This will most likely reveal the core of the root causes of the problem.

6. As a rule of thumb, this method often requires five rounds of the question "Why?"

An Example of the Use of Five Whys

As a small business in the rapidly growing field of Web site design and programming, an enterprise of about 25 people had grown from a small, home-based outfit into the current company with many large companies as clients. Previously, the team of programmers had received much acclaim for its Web page designs and innovative use of graphics that made sites easy to navigate. Lately, however, more and more clients were dissatisfied with the Web sites. They complained about functionality, simple errors in layout or text, late completion of designs and entire sites, and so on.

The situation had gotten to a point where the employees faced more and more problems and no longer thought the work was as much fun as it used to be. Some of the most entrenched technological freaks blamed the problems on the company's unwillingness to stay abreast of current developments; others thought most of the problems stemmed from a lack of qualified programmers.

To get to the bottom of these problems, which were threatening the future of the company, one of the founding partners used the five whys tool. The resulting chart is shown on the following page. As you can see, the root cause was neither of those previously believed to be the culprit, but rather too many projects being undertaken simultaneously.

FIVE WHYS EXAMPLE—WEB DESIGN COMPANY

Dissatisfied Web site customers

Why?   Lacking functionality

    Why?   Poor customer communication

        Why?   Too much time pressure

            Why?   Too many projects

Problem Solving
Root Cause Analysis
Problem Understanding
Problem Cause Brainstorming
Problem Cause Data Collection
Problem Cause Data Analysis
Root Cause Identification
Root Cause Elimination
Solution Implementation
Tool Selection
Example Cases

Problem Solving

Root Cause
Analysis

Problem
Understanding

Problem Cause
Brainstorming

Problem Cause
Data Collection

Problem Cause
Data Analysis

**Root Cause
Identification**

Root Cause
Elimination

Solution
Implementation

Tool Selection

Example Cases

CHECKLIST FOR FIVE WHYS

❑ Define a clear starting point for the analysis, either a problem or an identified cause at some level.

❑ Use brainstorming or other idea-generation approaches to find causes at the level below the starting point.

❑ For each identified cause, question whether it is a cause of the original problem. This process in turn generates new causes.

❑ Depict the chain of causes as a sequence of text on a whiteboard.

❑ For each new answer to the why question, pose the question again until no new answers result.

❑ This last cause (or causes) is the problem's root cause(s).

FIVE WHYS TEMPLATE

Why?

Why?

Why?

Why?

Why?

Problem Solving

Root Cause
Analysis

Problem
Understanding

Problem Cause
Brainstorming

Problem Cause
Data Collection

Problem Cause
Data Analysis

**Root Cause
Identification**

Root Cause
Elimination

Solution
Implementation

Tool Selection

Example Cases

Problem Solving

Root Cause
Analysis

Problem
Understanding

Problem Cause
Brainstorming

Problem Cause
Data Collection

Problem Cause
Data Analysis

**Root Cause
Identification**

Root Cause
Elimination

Solution
Implementation

Tool Selection

Example Cases

THE PURPOSE AND APPLICATIONS OF FAULT TREE ANALYSIS

The tools presented so far for generating ideas about possible causes have in common that they tend to treat all possible causes as equal and as isolated elements. The fact is that in many situations causes are related or belong to groups of similar issues.

Fault tree analysis is useful for portraying all possible causes in one diagram and identifying such links and naturally builds on the results from five whys analysis. Its purpose is to:

* Produce a clear overview of the possible causes identified.

* See linkages between causes or identify groups of related causes.

Fault Tree Analysis Is a Variant of the FMA Family of Tools

As we mentioned when discussing proactive problem prevention versus reactive problem solving, there is a family of tools for failure mode analysis (FMA). Various permutations of the basic tool take into account effects, criticalities, and so on. Common to these is that they are aimed at foreseeing what could go wrong, thus allowing products, systems, processes, and so on, to be designed in a way that either minimizes the risk of failures occurring or reduces the consequences should they occur.

Fault tree analysis is also a variant of an FMA tool that uses a specific type of tree diagram to portray the different failure modes. As with the other FMA-type tools, it can be used as a foresight tool to understand possible ways things can go wrong. It can also be used for after-the-fact analysis of problems that have already occurred, which is the application we have in mind when including it in this book and this chapter.

THE STEPS IN FAULT TREE ANALYSIS

1. Identify the problem to be analyzed and place it at the top of the tree diagram (this is the *top event*).

2. Brainstorm immediate causes at the level below the top event and plot these on the diagram respectively.

3. For each cause identified, assess whether it is the result of lower-level causes or represents a basic cause. Draw circles around basic causes not to be developed further and draw rectangles around intermediate causes.

4. For each that is not a basic cause, repeat steps 2 and 3 until the tree diagram contains only basic causes at the lowest level of each branch.

5. In the case of more than one cause leading to the level above, use symbols to connect the branches in the diagram to indicate whether these operate together (*and*, symbolized by ◓) or on their own (*or*, symbolized by ▲).

An Example of the Use of Fault Tree Analysis

When the Web design company from the five whys example realized that many of their problems were caused by taking on too many assignments at the same time, a whole new area of causes was opened up. The five whys analysis was followed up with fault tree analysis, both to generate further causes of the problems and relate these to each other.

The next page shows the resulting fault tree, which helped the company to understand that several different causes contributed to the problem:

- Too many projects taken on

- No good project management system in place

- Poor organization of resources and work

Problem Solving

Root Cause Analysis

Problem Understanding

Problem Cause Brainstorming

Problem Cause Data Collection

Problem Cause Data Analysis

Root Cause Identification

Root Cause Elimination

Solution Implementation

Tool Selection

Example Cases

Problem Solving

Root Cause
Analysis

Problem
Understanding

Problem Cause
Brainstorming

Problem Cause
Data Collection

Problem Cause
Data Analysis

**Root Cause
Identification**

Root Cause
Elimination

Solution
Implementation

Tool Selection

Example Cases

FAULT TREE ANALYSIS EXAMPLE—
WEB DESIGN COMPANY

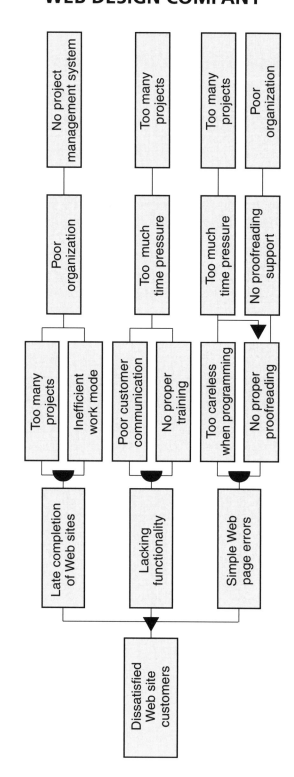

CHECKLIST FOR FAULT TREE ANALYSIS

❏ Define and place the top event at the top of the diagram to be developed.

❏ Brainstorm first-level causes below the top event and plot these on the fault tree to form the upper branches.

❏ Examine each cause at the different levels of the tree to determine whether it is a basic cause or the result of underlying causes.

❏ As underlying causes are identified, place these in the right position on the fault tree.

❏ Use "and" and "or" symbols to indicate how causes at the same level relate to each other when leading to the element above.

Problem Solving

Root Cause Analysis

Problem Understanding

Problem Cause Brainstorming

Problem Cause Data Collection

Problem Cause Data Analysis

Root Cause Identification

Root Cause Elimination

Solution Implementation

Tool Selection

Example Cases

Problem Solving

Root Cause
Analysis

Problem
Understanding

Problem Cause
Brainstorming

Problem Cause
Data Collection

Problem Cause
Data Analysis

**Root Cause
Identification**

Root Cause
Elimination

Solution
Implementation

Tool Selection

Example Cases

FAULT TREE ANALYSIS TEMPLATE

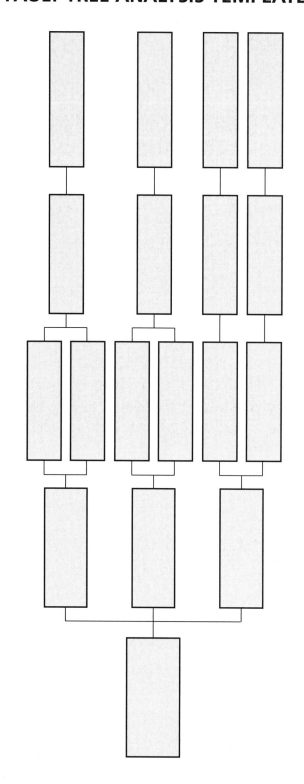

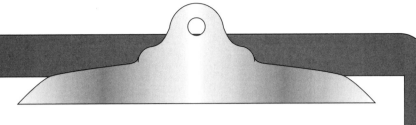

ROOT CAUSE IDENTIFICATION CHECKLIST

Although root cause analysis is not one clear process from start to finish, some distinct stages are discernible. This checklist helps assess whether the most important elements of the root cause identification stage have been accomplished before moving on.

❑ Use the results of the problem cause data analysis stage to determine the starting point for the root cause identification stage.

❑ Assess the identified possible causes to determine which tool to use. Consider the number of causes found, the degree of similarity between them, the extent to which some of them seem to stand out as obvious root causes, and so on.

❑ Choose among the following analysis tools: matrix diagrams, cause-and-effect charts, five whys, and fault tree analysis.

❑ Carry out the analysis according to the steps of the selected tool or tools.

❑ The conclusions from the root cause identification stage should be true and relevant conclusions about the root cause of the problem being analyzed.

Problem Solving

Root Cause Analysis

Problem Understanding

Problem Cause Brainstorming

Problem Cause Data Collection

Problem Cause Data Analysis

Root Cause Identification

Root Cause Elimination

Solution Implementation

Tool Selection

Example Cases

8

Tools for Root Cause Elimination

This chapter deals with devising solutions to the problem by eliminating the root cause. As in the preceding chapter, there are techniques available for this purpose that are rather complex and deserve more extensive coverage than that given to each tool in this book. We have therefore chosen to include one approach to stimulating creativity when looking for new solutions, the six thinking hats, and two tools for developing solutions, the theory of inventive problem solving (TRIZ) and systematic inventive thinking (SIT).

Problem Solving

Root Cause Analysis

Problem Understanding

Problem Cause Brainstorming

Problem Cause Data Collection

Problem Cause Data Analysis

Root Cause Identification

Root Cause Elimination

Solution Implementation

Tool Selection

Example Cases

Problem Solving
Root Cause Analysis
Problem Understanding
Problem Cause Brainstorming
Problem Cause Data Collection
Problem Cause Data Analysis
Root Cause Identification
Root Cause Elimination
Solution Implementation
Tool Selection
Example Cases

ROOT CAUSE ELIMINATION

If you're ready to breathe a sigh of relief and relax the problem-solving effort after having completed the root cause identification stage, think again. Your project is not at its end until the root cause has been eliminated by finding a solution to the problem.

While the previous phases have been characterized by analytical efforts to understand the problem and its possible causes, finding a solution is a more creative effort.

There are many tools suitable for this task, but those presented in this book are:

- The six thinking hats

- The theory of inventive problem solving (TRIZ)

- Systematic inventive thinking (SIT)

Sometimes You Need to Remind Your Customers

Many auto repair shops frequently experience customers simply forgetting their appointments and failing to show up. This causes the assigned mechanic to either be out of work for the allotted period of time or having to find other tasks, as well as having to reschedule the appointment for the customer.

One company saw this problem occurring so often, they decided to try to do something about it. Analyzing the problem, it quickly became clear that the root cause was nothing more complicated than the human being's forgetfulness. Even when customers penciled the appointments into their various calendars, typically on the fridge or other similar calendars without any reminder function like PDAs have, they forgot.

A small team pondered the problem for a while, considering sending appointment letters to the customers, for example. This had, however, been a standard practice some years ago, and there had been a problem with sending the letter at the right time. Too early and the customers forgot anyway, too late and the letter arrived on the actual day of the appointment.

At around the same time, a new switchboard was installed. It was far more advanced than the old one, allowing cell phone hookup, meeting scheduling with phone reminders to employees, and so on. It turned out that with a small additional software module, the system could auto-generate text messages, for example to customers. The software was purchased, installed, and tweaked to this purpose, and soon it was able to send automatic reminders to customers the day before their appointment.

Four months after implementing the system, no-show customers had dropped to one-tenth of the previous level.

THE PURPOSE AND APPLICATIONS OF THE SIX THINKING HATS

The purpose of the so-called six thinking hats is to actively encourage people to view a problem and its solutions from several different perspectives. Deliberately having a team member take the position of devil's advocate ensures that suggested solutions are debated with regard to feasibility and possible flaws.

The technique achieves this by encouraging you to recognize what type of thinking you are using, and to apply different types of thinking to the subject.

In root cause analysis, applications of the six thinking hats are:

- Viewing problems and solutions from different perspectives

- Ensuring that they are subjected to close scrutiny before decisions are made

---

The Six Thinking Hats

Created by Edward de Bono when working to improve creativity and lateral thinking, the six thinking hats were given the following colors and respective roles:

- *The white hat.* Cold, neutral, and objective, the person "wearing" it should be systematic and careful in looking at the facts and figures.

- *The red hat.* Represents anger, the wearer should make sure she or he listens to intuition/gut feeling and their own emotions.

- *The black hat.* Pessimistic and negative, thinking with this hat on should focus on why an idea will fail.

- *The yellow hat.* Optimistic, sunny, and positive, focusing on seeing ways ideas will work and trying to overcome obstacles.

- *The green hat.* Represents grass, fertility, and growth; the person underneath it should be creative and try to cultivate new ideas.

- *The blue hat.* Connected with the sky, focusing on seeing things from a higher perspective.

Although some of the connotations used in describing the hats can be construed as negative, it is important to understand that each hat is equally important in ensuring fruitful discussions.

Problem Solving

Root Cause Analysis

Problem Understanding

Problem Cause Brainstorming

Problem Cause Data Collection

Problem Cause Data Analysis

Root Cause Identification

Root Cause Elimination

Solution Implementation

Tool Selection

Example Cases

THE STEPS IN USING THE SIX THINKING HATS

1. Assign hats to the people on the discussion team, preferably one color per person, and make sure that everybody understands that when speaking during the session, they must clearly identify with the color of their hat.

2. The team engages in a creative discussion about the problem, with the following main responsibilities (other team members can of course also contribute at each step):

3. The facts about the problem are presented by the white hat.

4. The green hat presents ideas on how the problem could be solved.

5. The possible solutions are discussed, with the yellow hat focusing on benefits, the black hat on drawbacks.

6. The red hat works to elicit all team members' gut feelings about the solutions.

7. The blue hat summarizes the discussion and closes the meeting.

An Example of the Use of the Six Thinking Hats

In March 1996, the Creutzfeldt-Jakob disease, also known as mad cow disease, spread rapidly throughout Europe, creating panic about beef and dramatically reducing its consumption. Many beef processing plants experienced huge overnight losses as consumers stopped buying beef.

One of Europe's largest beef processing companies experienced an 86 percent loss of turnover overnight. Not surprisingly, it was an extremely difficult task to try to think in such circumstances. Managers were fully occupied coping with the sudden loss of business.

Twelve people from this company met for a 60-minute meeting using the six thinking hats. Sixty-five ideas were generated—30 cost-reduction ideas and 35 commercial ideas. They were evaluated using the yellow hat and black hat processes at subsequent meetings.

As a result, 25 ideas were implemented. For example, major capital investment was directed toward a new plant participating in the Government OTMS program (*over thirty month slaughter*, an effort to prevent cattle older than 30 months from entering the human food chain). The in-house-only distribution division refocused and became open-market commercial, being so successful that it has had to expand to cope with all the business received.

The overall result is that they came through the crisis with a strong company and survived six long weeks of no revenue.

CHECKLIST FOR THE
SIX THINKING HATS

❏ Make sure that the concept of the six thinking hats is fully understood by everyone, especially the fact that participants should actively try to think as someone else, not their usual selves.

❏ Assign the six hats, preferably to six different people or more.

❏ Discuss the problem actively using the six thinking hats and their associated roles.

❏ List benefits and drawbacks of suggested solutions and discuss these using the yellow and black hats.

❏ Summarize the discussion coherently by the blue hat.

Problem Solving

Root Cause Analysis

Problem Understanding

Problem Cause Brainstorming

Problem Cause Data Collection

Problem Cause Data Analysis

Root Cause Identification

Root Cause Elimination

Solution Implementation

Tool Selection

Example Cases

Problem Solving

Root Cause
Analysis

Problem
Understanding

Problem Cause
Brainstorming

Problem Cause
Data Collection

Problem Cause
Data Analysis

Root Cause
Identification

**Root Cause
Elimination**

Solution
Implementation

Tool Selection

Example Cases

THE PURPOSE AND APPLICATIONS OF TRIZ

TRIZ was developed for solving problems, mainly engineering problems, requiring solutions that go beyond simply applying known solutions to similar problems. These problems are termed *inventive problems* and often require the combined knowledge of different disciplines to produce a solution.

The main purpose of TRIZ is to allow problem solvers to dissect the problem into its core components and free themselves from known solutions, thus venturing into the territory of truly novel solutions.

In root cause analysis, TRIZ can be used to:

- Generally stimulate the creativity of the team conducting the analysis.

- Find solutions to the problem in question.

The History of TRIZ

Genrich S. Altshuller, born in the former Soviet Union in 1926, worked in the Soviet Navy as a patent expert in the 1940s. Altshuller screened over 200,000 patents looking for inventive problems (defined as a problem in which the solution causes another problem to appear, such as when increasing the strength of a metal plate causes its weight to increase) and how they were solved. Of these, only 40,000 had somewhat inventive solutions; the rest were straightforward improvements. Usually, inventors must resort to a tradeoff or compromise between features and thus do not achieve an ideal solution. In his study of patents, Altshuller found that many described a solution that eliminated or resolved such contradictions and required no tradeoff.

Altshuller categorized these patents by looking beyond the industries they originated from and found that often the same problems had been solved over and over again using one of only 40 fundamental inventive principles. Eventually, Altshuller tabulated that over 90 percent of the problems engineers faced had been solved somewhere before.

For example, one problem in using artificial diamonds for tool making is that cutting methods often result in new fractures which do not appear until the diamond is in use. A method is used in food canning to split green peppers and remove the seeds, based on using air pressure in a hermetic chamber, causing the peppers to shrink and fracture at the stem, then burst at the weakest point and eject the seed pod. A similar technique was applied to the diamond cutting process, resulting in the crystals splitting along their natural fracture lines with no additional damage.

Altshuller distilled the problems, contradictions, and solutions in these patents into a theory of inventive problem solving which he named TRIZ.

THE STEPS IN USING TRIZ

1. Identify the problem and its operating environment, resource requirements, primary useful function, harmful effects, and ideal result.

2. Formulate the problem more precisely, using the so-called prism of TRIZ to focus on physical contradictions.

3. Search for a previously well-solved problem, based on 39 standard technical characteristics that cause conflict (termed engineering parameters), first finding the principle that needs to be changed, then the principle that is an undesirable secondary effect.

4. Look for analogous solutions and adapt them to the problem, based on the 40 inventive principles, producing hints that will help an engineer find an inventive solution. Altshuller tabulated the 39 engineering parameters against the appropriate inventive principles to use for a solution to aid this step (see for example http://www.mazur.net/triz/contradi.htm).

Problem Solving

Root Cause Analysis

Problem Understanding

Problem Cause Brainstorming

Problem Cause Data Collection

Problem Cause Data Analysis

Root Cause Identification

Root Cause Elimination

Solution Implementation

Tool Selection

Example Cases

An Example of the Use of TRIZ

Beverage cans are used in an operating environment where they are stacked for storage purposes. Harmful effects include the costs of materials and producing the can and waste of storage space. The ideal is a can that can support the weight of stacking to human height without damage to the cans or the beverage inside the cans.

The manufacturer cannot control the height to which cans will be stacked. The price of raw materials compels them to lower costs by making the walls thinner. If the manufacturer makes the walls thinner, they cannot support as large a stacking load. The physical contradiction is thus that the can walls need to be thinner to lower the material cost and thicker to support the stacking-load weight.

The standard engineering parameter that has to be changed to make the can wall thinner is #4 "length of a nonmoving object," length here meaning thickness. If the manufactuer makes the wall thinner, the stacking-load weight will decrease, and the standard engineering parameter that is in conflict is #11 "stress."

The feature to improve is the can wall thickness (#4 "length of a nonmoving object") and the undesirable secondary effect is loss of load bearing capacity (#11 "stress"). Looking these up in the Table of Contradictions, we find the inventive principles 1c, 14a, and 35:

Continued

Continued

Problem Solving

Root Cause Analysis

Problem Understanding

Problem Cause Brainstorming

Problem Cause Data Collection

Problem Cause Data Analysis

Root Cause Identification

Root Cause Elimination

Solution Implementation

Tool Selection

Example Cases

- Inventive Principle 1c—Increase the degree of an object's segmentation: the wall of the can could be changed from one smooth continuous wall to a corrugated surface made up of many "little walls" to increase the edge strength of the wall yet allow a thinner material to be used.

- Inventive Principle 14a—Replace linear parts or flat surfaces with curved ones: the perpendicular angle at which most can lids are welded to the can wall can be changed to a curve.

- Inventive Principle 35—Transform the physical and chemical states of an object: changing the can's composition to a stronger metal alloy will increase the load bearing capacity.

In less than one week, utilizing these techniques, inventor Jim Kowalik of Renaissance Leadership Institute was able to propose over 20 usable solutions to this problem to the U.S. canned beverage industry, several which have been adopted.

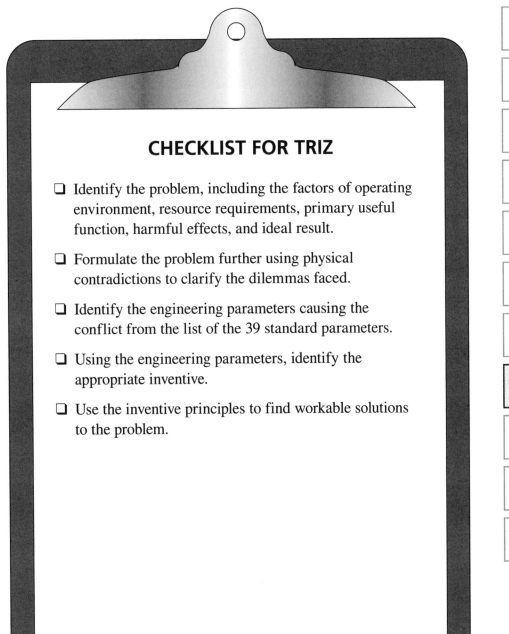

CHECKLIST FOR TRIZ

❑ Identify the problem, including the factors of operating environment, resource requirements, primary useful function, harmful effects, and ideal result.

❑ Formulate the problem further using physical contradictions to clarify the dilemmas faced.

❑ Identify the engineering parameters causing the conflict from the list of the 39 standard parameters.

❑ Using the engineering parameters, identify the appropriate inventive.

❑ Use the inventive principles to find workable solutions to the problem.

Problem Solving

Root Cause Analysis

Problem Understanding

Problem Cause Brainstorming

Problem Cause Data Collection

Problem Cause Data Analysis

Root Cause Identification

Root Cause Elimination

Solution Implementation

Tool Selection

Example Cases

Problem Solving

Root Cause Analysis

Problem Understanding

Problem Cause Brainstorming

Problem Cause Data Collection

Problem Cause Data Analysis

Root Cause Identification

Root Cause Elimination

Solution Implementation

Tool Selection

Example Cases

THE PURPOSE AND APPLICATIONS OF SIT

SIT can be seen as a further development of TRIZ, both enhancing the steps of the technique and adapting it to working in "fuzzier" areas such as new product development and other more creative processes.

SIT is based on the principle of the "closed world," stating that a creative solution to a problem relies mainly on the natural components in the world of the problem or its neighboring environment.

In root cause analysis, SIT can be used to:

* Find creative solutions to problems.

* Ensure that these solutions are workable and belong to the environment of the problem, thus making them easier to implement.

Main Principles of SIT

Pioneered by Israelis Jacob Goldberger and David Mazursky, systematic inventive thinking has been developed by several researchers as well as companies applying the technique. As a result, there is some variation with regard to the key principles used to stimulate the creative problem-solving process. According to Goldberger and Mazursky, there are five such principles:

* *Attribute dependency,* the most widely used template, considers changing a key variable of a product. For instance, why couldn't wet diapers generate a strong but pleasant scent—instead of the usual one—to let parents know the baby needs a change?

* *Component control* looks at the way a product is linked with its environment. Post-It Notes might have been this template's answer to the question, "How can memo writers link their notes to the place where they want them to be seen?"

* *Replacement* is substituting part of a product with something from the product's immediate environment. Using this template, a manufacturer trying to reduce the size of a car cell phone speaker could remove the unit's dedicated speaker and use the car's radio speaker instead. This not only eliminates the extra speaker, it improves the telephone's sound.

* *Displacement* considers improving a product's performance by removing an intrinsic component. More than 20 years ago, Sony Corporation realized it could squeeze high-quality playback into its early Walkmans if it removed the recording function.

* *Division* simply aims to split one product's attributes into two, like the separation of shampoo from conditioner.

THE STEPS IN USING SIT

1. Assemble a team representing all the knowledge possibly relevant to the problem in question, perhaps with as many as 10 to 12 members.

2. List all the components of the closed world of the problem, making sure to include components that might seem irrelevant.

3. Use the five SIT principles in sequence on the components to develop numerous ideas for problem solutions, employing sentences of the type, "An *X* type of component from the closed world will be used to prevent the problem from occurring."

4. Assess the ideas generated and select those best suited for further elaboration.

5. Keep fleshing out the most promising ideas and developing one or more solutions that contain more detail.

| Problem Solving |
| Root Cause Analysis |
| Problem Understanding |
| Problem Cause Brainstorming |
| Problem Cause Data Collection |
| Problem Cause Data Analysis |
| Root Cause Identification |
| **Root Cause Elimination** |
| Solution Implementation |
| Tool Selection |
| Example Cases |

An Example of the Use of SIT

Oceangoing ships face challenges in handling the gradual build-up of so-called bilge sludge during voyages. This is a waste product consisting of water, oil, and other substances, and discharging it into the ocean is prohibited or strictly regulated. As a result, vessels must have tanks to store the bilge sludge onboard until they can offload it safely when in harbor. The problem is of course that the tanks claim space that could be used for better purposes, including carrying more cargo or reducing the ship's size and thus fuel consumption.

Using the SIT approach, a team of people from a shipping company, with varying expertise, attacked this intrinsic problem. Through a combination of the replacement and displacement principles, the rough idea was formulated to use the fuel tanks in some way for storing the bilge sludge. Analyzing the question further, it seemed clear that the gradual depletion of the fuel tanks was faster than the gradual build-up of bilge sludge, thus making it feasible to utilize the spare volume in the fuel tanks for this purpose.

The technical details on how to get this to work in practice have yet to be hammered out, but it is believed that some sort of flexible membrane producing a two-chamber effect in the fuel tanks could work. This way, bilge sludge could be pumped into the tanks from the top as fuel is consumed, completely solving the problem of needing dedicated tanks for this waste product. In addition to improving the space utilization of the vessels, it would also prevent ships from being tempted into illegally discharging the bilge sludge into the sea.

Problem Solving

Root Cause
Analysis

Problem
Understanding

Problem Cause
Brainstorming

Problem Cause
Data Collection

Problem Cause
Data Analysis

Root Cause
Identification

**Root Cause
Elimination**

Solution
Implementation

Tool Selection

Example Cases

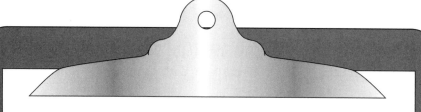

CHECKLIST FOR SIT

❑ Assemble a team containing members with a broad range of expertise related to the problem.

❑ Identify and list all the components present in the closed world of the problem.

❑ Apply each of the five SIT principles to the components of the closed world to generate ideas for new solutions.

❑ Analyze the list of ideas to identify the most promising ones.

❑ Develop further the most promising ideas to render more detailed solutions.

ROOT CAUSE ELIMINATION CHECKLIST

Although root cause analysis is not one clear process from start to finish, some distinct stages are discernible. This checklist helps assess whether the most important elements of the root cause elimination stage have been accomplished before moving on.

❑ Use the results of the root cause identification stage to determine the starting point for the root cause elimination stage.

❑ Consider the root cause identified as the heart of the problem and to what extent either creativity or structured engineering analysis are required to eliminate it.

❑ Choose among the following tools for eliminating the root case: the six thinking hats, TRIZ, or SIT.

❑ Use the selected technique or techniques to create one or more solutions that will eliminate the root cause.

❑ The conclusions from the root cause elimination stage should be workable solutions to the problem being studied, which are then brought forward to the solution implementation stage.

Problem Solving

Root Cause Analysis

Problem Understanding

Problem Cause Brainstorming

Problem Cause Data Collection

Problem Cause Data Analysis

Root Cause Identification

Root Cause Elimination

Solution Implementation

Tool Selection

Example Cases

9

Tools for Solution Implementation

Problem Solving

Root Cause Analysis

Problem Understanding

Problem Cause Brainstorming

Problem Cause Data Collection

Problem Cause Data Analysis

Root Cause Identification

Root Cause Elimination

Solution Implementation

Tool Selection

Example Cases

As the last chapter presenting tools and techniques, this chapter is about finally implementing the changes that are required to reach a lasting solution to the problem being dealt with. As opposed to the previous chapters, this one also includes more general advice in addition to specific techniques.

Problem Solving

Root Cause
Analysis

Problem
Understanding

Problem Cause
Brainstorming

Problem Cause
Data Collection

Problem Cause
Data Analysis

Root Cause
Identification

Root Cause
Elimination

**Solution
Implementation**

Tool Selection

Example Cases

SOLUTION IMPLEMENTATION

So far, the focus of this book has been on identifying and eliminating the root cause, and little has been said about how to make changes happen in the organization. We will now focus on the implementation phase, which includes:

- Organizing the implementation

- Developing an implementation plan

- Creating acceptance of the required changes and a favorable climate for the implementation.

- Carrying out the implementation itself

The tools used in this phase are:

- Tree diagram

- Force-field analysis

Follow Through

It is vital to complete the cycle in root cause analysis, implementing the solution in a thorough way. In many organizations, we have experienced a clear lack of follow-through in this phase. People tend to focus their attention on new and more exciting projects, rather than finishing the old ones. This is by no means surprising or illogical; solving the problem is always more fun than the hard work of implementing the solution.

Keep in mind, though, that implementation plans lying around in drawers or computer folders do nothing to eliminate the problem. One way to overcome this lack of follow-through is to award some kind of bonus to the team that sees the implementation all the way to the finish line. Additionally, some sort of performance measurement system to track implementation progress, not to mention the performance of the resulting problem-free business process, can help in keeping focus.

ORGANIZING THE IMPLEMENTATION

There are several alternatives available when it comes to deciding how the implementation should be organized:

- By the original improvement team

- By a specific implementation team

- In the line organization

A word on the importance of change agents is also justified. In any organization, some people are more visible or outspoken than others. They might not be leaders in the formal sense, but in practice, they lead others by their informal position and actions. Some of these people should be included in the implementation team in order to enhance its acceptance and to minimize grapevine rumors concerning the project.

Three Alternatives

Three main alternatives for organizing the implementation are:

- By the original improvement team, where the same team that has carried out the project so far also undertakes the implementation of improvements. The advantage of this approach is that the team knows the project and what the solutions entail.

- By a specific implementation team, where a new team is formed consisting of the necessary and suitable persons to assume the responsibility for the implementation itself. Even if this team does not know the work so far, for the implementation it is often wise to use, or at least include, other persons than those who were involved in the development of the improvement proposals. The advantage of this approach is that people with particular authority or credibility in the organization can be handpicked for the team.

- In the line organization, where the functionally responsible persons assume responsibility for implementing the changes by using the resources of the ordinary organization. This is perhaps the most common model, where we ensure that those who will later work in the changed business process also take part in implementing it.

Problem Solving

Root Cause Analysis

Problem Understanding

Problem Cause Brainstorming

Problem Cause Data Collection

Problem Cause Data Analysis

Root Cause Identification

Root Cause Elimination

Solution Implementation

Tool Selection

Example Cases

Problem Solving

Root Cause
Analysis

Problem
Understanding

Problem Cause
Brainstorming

Problem Cause
Data Collection

Problem Cause
Data Analysis

Root Cause
Identification

Root Cause
Elimination

**Solution
Implementation**

Tool Selection

Example Cases

DEVELOPING AN IMPLEMENTATION PLAN

Generally, an implementation plan should cover the following elements:

- *Required activities.* Activities that need to be carried out to implement the improvement proposals generated in the problem-solving process.

- *Activity sequence.* The order in which the activities must be carried out.

- *Organization and responsibility.* An indication of who is responsible for both carrying out and monitoring the progress of each activity.

- *Schedule.* A more detailed plan for when the activities should be carried out, including milestones for key results expected throughout the project.

- *Costs.* Estimates of the costs involved in the implementation.

Setting Targets

The implementation plan should set targets for the solution implementation. These targets should be ambitious but still possible to attain. In order to commit fully to such targets, the organization should define some kind of ownership for the targets. The improvement group should thus involve some of the employees in this process.

Too ambitious targets can lead to frustration and disillusionment, spreading a feeling in the organization that the goals can never be reached. This might be management's way of communicating to the employees that they should always reach higher. However, our experience is that this might not always succeed. If the employees have a feeling that the ambitions are out of reach, they might become less motivated.

Too low ambitions can be equally damaging. Very often, a target also acts as a ceiling of performance, meaning there are few mechanisms to make people reach higher than the defined target. Thus, we often see projects reaching their targets but very seldom going beyond them. If the targets are set too low, they will be easy to reach and certainly not tap into the full potential of the organization.

THE PURPOSE AND APPLICATIONS OF TREE DIAGRAMS

There are several different techniques for project planning, involving different levels of scope and complexity. One quite easy-to-use tool, suitable for breaking down larger tasks into activities of a manageable size, is a tree diagram. Implementation processes can be complex matters, and forcing oneself to structure the activities with such a diagram is a very good start at breaking down and organizing the work.

In root cause analysis, the main uses of tree diagrams are to:

- Structure complex tasks into logical activities.

- Plan the implementation process of the solution.

More Complex Project Planning

Tree diagrams are really "cheating" compared with what project managers would call project planning. There are several far more complex approaches available, ranging from network planning using deterministic estimates of activity durations to using statistical functions to model such durations. In the latter case, different analyses can be performed that calculate the most likely length of activities, determine the most likely critical path of activities, and allow for making contingency plans.

As the figure below shows, a typical tree diagram will represent a hierarchy of activities. The main activities, read from left to right in the diagram, represent the main tasks of the implementation. These main tasks will often be artificial activities, that is, names of a group of subactivities. Each of these main activities will therefore generally include a number of subactivities below them, to be carried out in the order they are presented, from left to right.

Information about deadlines, responsibility, costs, and so on, can be attached to each activity in the diagram.

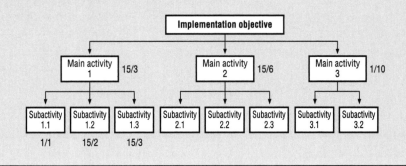

Problem Solving

Root Cause Analysis

Problem Understanding

Problem Cause Brainstorming

Problem Cause Data Collection

Problem Cause Data Analysis

Root Cause Identification

Root Cause Elimination

Solution Implementation

Tool Selection

Example Cases

THE STEPS IN USING TREE DIAGRAMS

1. Generate a list of activities that must be performed to implement the solution.

2. Write down each activity, in the form of a verb followed by a noun, on adhesive notes.

3. Arrange the activities in logical subgroups of activities that must be performed in sequence.

4. Arrange the subgroups into an overall sequence to illustrate the entire plan of the tree diagram.

An Example of the Use of Tree Diagrams

A library decided to introduce a new computer-based registration system. To plan this task, the employees designed the tree diagram shown below. For each activity, the date by which it should be completed was attached.

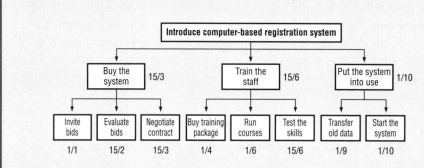

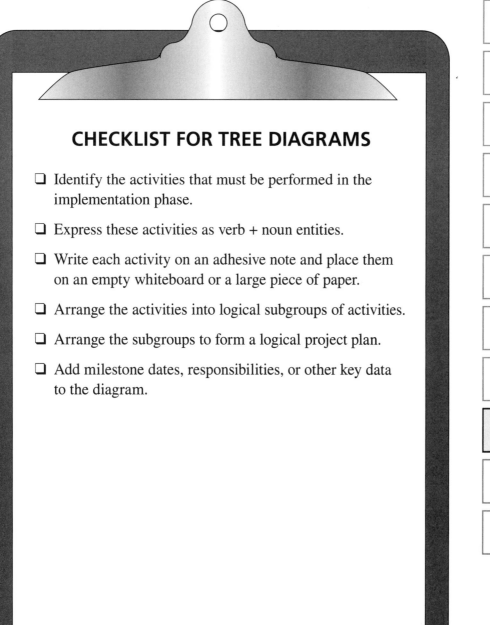

CHECKLIST FOR TREE DIAGRAMS

❑ Identify the activities that must be performed in the implementation phase.

❑ Express these activities as verb + noun entities.

❑ Write each activity on an adhesive note and place them on an empty whiteboard or a large piece of paper.

❑ Arrange the activities into logical subgroups of activities.

❑ Arrange the subgroups to form a logical project plan.

❑ Add milestone dates, responsibilities, or other key data to the diagram.

Problem Solving

Root Cause Analysis

Problem Understanding

Problem Cause Brainstorming

Problem Cause Data Collection

Problem Cause Data Analysis

Root Cause Identification

Root Cause Elimination

Solution Implementation

Tool Selection

Example Cases

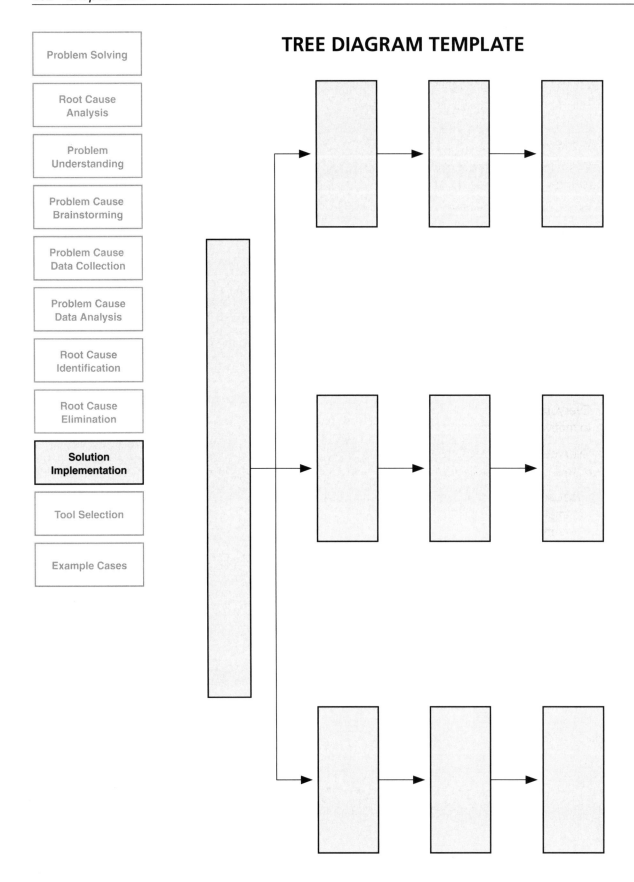

TREE DIAGRAM TEMPLATE

CREATING CHANGE ACCEPTANCE

One of the subtasks in the implementation phase is to create acceptance of the suggested changes and a favorable climate for their implementation. This is in itself not an insignificant task and involves fields such as psychology, human resource management, and so on.

A general observation in change situations is that the more information that is given to those who will be affected by the changes, the less resistance will be met. Thus, communicating the consequences of the changes to everyone affected and others that might represent obstacles to an effective implementation is a good strategy.

Those Affected By the Changes

Typical stakeholders to consider are:

- Top management, which has the authority to decide on implementation and allotting the necessary resources for it

- Everyone involved in the process to be changed, as it is essential to motivate them for the change

- Everyone delivering input into to the process or receiving output from it, as they could also be affected by the changes

- Other so-called gatekeepers, that is, persons who can impact the implementation and its progress, often persons with financial authority

An implementation situation is like a low pressure system—it sucks up rumors from all around it—so feed the organization with pertinent and timely information to avoid the grapevine growing hot.

Problem Solving
Root Cause Analysis
Problem Understanding
Problem Cause Brainstorming
Problem Cause Data Collection
Problem Cause Data Analysis
Root Cause Identification
Root Cause Elimination
Solution Implementation
Tool Selection
Example Cases

Problem Solving

Root Cause
Analysis

Problem
Understanding

Problem Cause
Brainstorming

Problem Cause
Data Collection

Problem Cause
Data Analysis

Root Cause
Identification

Root Cause
Elimination

**Solution
Implementation**

Tool Selection

Example Cases

THE PURPOSE AND APPLICATIONS OF FORCE-FIELD ANALYSIS

When it comes to creating a positive climate for ensuing changes, force-field analysis is a helpful tool that can contribute to creating an overview of the situation and possible actions to improve it. Force-field analysis is based on the assumption that any situation is the result of forces for and against the current state, which are in equilibrium with each other. An increase or decrease in the strength of some of the forces will induce a change, a fact that can be used to create changes in the desired direction.

In root cause analysis, force-field analysis can be used to:

• Gain insight into the change climate of an implementation.

• Plan effective implementation activities.

$E = Q \times A!$

Often we see that implementation efforts fail, and those involved wonder why, as the objectives often are impeccable. It has been suggested (by others than ourselves) that the efficiency of the change (termed E) is a result of the following formula

$$E = Q \times A$$

where Q is the quality of the change approach and A is the level of acceptance for the change in the stakeholders.

Research has shown that:

• 98 percent of unsuccessful change projects have high Q!

• All successful change projects have high Q and high A!

THE STEPS IN USING FORCE-FIELD ANALYSIS

1. Define clearly what change is desired, information that can usually be taken directly from the implementation plan and its improvement objectives.

2. Brainstorm all possible forces in the organization that could be expected to work for or against the change.

3. Assess the strength of each of the forces and plot them on a force-field diagram. The length of each arrow in the diagram expresses the strength of the force it represents.

4. For each force, but especially the stronger ones, define actions that could increase the forces for the change or reduce those against it.

An Example of the Use of Force-Field Analysis

During a reorganization debate in the local branch of a major volunteer organization, the issue of a common economy came up. Currently a local branch of the organization has four departments, each with its own budget. Some argued that it should remain that way, while others argued that resources would be utilized better if they all shared a joint account.

As the temperature of the debate rose, it was suggested that a force-field analysis be used as a neutral tool to sketch the arguments for and against such a change. The result was the figure depicted below. Although the arguments for a change were important, it was decided not to change the current state, as the forces against dominated.

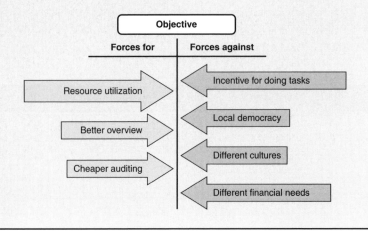

Problem Solving

Root Cause Analysis

Problem Understanding

Problem Cause Brainstorming

Problem Cause Data Collection

Problem Cause Data Analysis

Root Cause Identification

Root Cause Elimination

Solution Implementation

Tool Selection

Example Cases

Problem Solving

Root Cause
Analysis

Problem
Understanding

Problem Cause
Brainstorming

Problem Cause
Data Collection

Problem Cause
Data Analysis

Root Cause
Identification

Root Cause
Elimination

**Solution
Implementation**

Tool Selection

Example Cases

CHECKLIST FOR
FORCE-FIELD ANALYSIS

❑ Clearly define the change desired.

❑ Brainstorm all possible forces in the organization that could be expected to work for or against the change.

❑ Assess the strength of each of the forces.

❑ Place the forces in a force-field diagram, using the length of each arrow to represent the strength of the force.

❑ Define actions that could increase the forces for the change or reduce those against it.

FORCE-FIELD ANALYSIS TEMPLATE

Forces for	Forces against

Problem Solving

Root Cause
Analysis

Problem
Understanding

Problem Cause
Brainstorming

Problem Cause
Data Collection

Problem Cause
Data Analysis

Root Cause
Identification

Root Cause
Elimination

**Solution
Implementation**

Tool Selection

Example Cases

Problem Solving

Root Cause Analysis

Problem Understanding

Problem Cause Brainstorming

Problem Cause Data Collection

Problem Cause Data Analysis

Root Cause Identification

Root Cause Elimination

Solution Implementation

Tool Selection

Example Cases

CARRYING OUT THE IMPLEMENTATION ITSELF

Some last words about implementation:

- Involve everyone responsible for results from the process that is being improved to ensure full support for the changes.

- Try to elicit involvement and inspiration from those involved in the project.

- Follow a clearly communicated plan.

- Keep the affected persons constantly informed about progress and achieved results.

- Emphasize the importance of patience—changes do not happen overnight.

- Put the process under pressure—delays are common.

- Pick low-hanging fruit and celebrate wins.

A Sense of Crisis Can Be Useful

Research shows that if the organization feels there is some kind of crisis, the chances of a successful implementation process are enhanced. Reasons for a false sense of security might be the absence of a large and visible crisis, too many visible resources, low performance requirements, organizational structures that direct the employees' attention to narrow-minded functional objectives, internal measurement systems focused on the wrong issues, lack of feedback from external sources about performance levels and development, a culture of smoothing out conflicts, and too much "nice" feedback from management. Some ways to increase the sense of crisis can be:

- Create a crisis by allowing financial losses, revealing weaknesses compared to competitors, or letting errors be corrected at the very last second.

- Eliminate obvious sources of waste or luxury.

- Set targets for revenues, profits, or customer satisfaction so high that they cannot be achieved by doing things the same old way.

- Make customer satisfaction and performance data widely available.

- Insist that employees regularly talk to dissatisfied customers or suppliers.

- Bombard people with information about future opportunities and the benefits achievable through pursuing them.

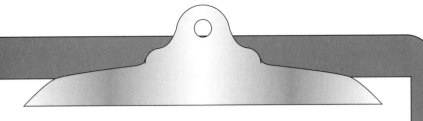

SOLUTION IMPLEMENTATION CHECKLIST

Although root cause analysis is not one clear process from start to finish, some distinct stages are discernible. This checklist helps assess whether the most important elements of the solution implementation stage have been accomplished before declaring the root cause analysis project completed.

❑ Use the results of the root cause elimination stage to determine the starting point for the solution implementation stage.

❑ Assess the solutions created in the previous phase.

❑ Discuss and determine how to organize the implementation task.

❑ Choose among the following tools for enabling the implementation of the solution: tree diagram or force-field analysis.

❑ Use the selected technique or techniques to create a favorable change climate and a feasible implementation plan.

❑ Implement the solution by executing the plan.

❑ Make sure the solution has been firmly rooted in the business processes and has removed the problem.

Problem Solving

Root Cause Analysis

Problem Understanding

Problem Cause Brainstorming

Problem Cause Data Collection

Problem Cause Data Analysis

Root Cause Identification

Root Cause Elimination

Solution Implementation

Tool Selection

Example Cases

10

How to Select the Right Tool

Problem Solving

Root Cause Analysis

Problem Understanding

Problem Cause Brainstorming

Problem Cause Data Collection

Problem Cause Data Analysis

Root Cause Identification

Root Cause Elimination

Solution Implementation

Tool Selection

Example Cases

Chapters 3 through 9 presented an abundance of different tools and techniques. It is difficult to know which tool should be used when, and how the tools relate to one another in an overall root cause analysis. This chapter gives advice and sets forth guidelines for selecting the appropriate tool in a given situation.

Problem Solving

Root Cause
Analysis

Problem
Understanding

Problem Cause
Brainstorming

Problem Cause
Data Collection

Problem Cause
Data Analysis

Root Cause
Identification

Root Cause
Elimination

Solution
Implementation

Tool Selection

Example Cases

A WORD OF CAUTION ABOUT TOOLS

Before looking into tool selection, consider this warning on the topic of tools. The main objective of your exercise is to find the root cause of your problem and eliminate it. The tools we've presented are mere aids that can help you reach this goal. Don't let your focus on tools blur your sight of the target! Too much emphasis on the tools can lead to the problem becoming secondary.

Two key recommendations are:

• Do not become a slave to one or more tools!

• Remember that a tool is not a solution in search of a problem to solve!

Master Many Tools

While it is not necessary to know every tool presented in this book, we urge you to acquaint yourself with several of them, enabling you to be flexible in applying them. Each tool has its strengths and weaknesses. The tool should fit the problem, not the other way around.

The old saying "many roads lead to Rome" also applies in problem solving. There seldom is only one right way of applying problem-solving techniques. Indeed, we have a number of options in terms of procedure and choice of tools. To be flexible, you should be able to use a variety of tools in solving problems. All too often people become slaves to one tool. This wastes time and energy and causes disillusionment.

TOOL SELECTION IN GENERAL

The guidelines for the selection of tools are based on a few parameters and should not be followed blindly. You, the reader, have considerable knowledge about the situation at hand and might find another tool more suitable. If the group agrees, then this other tool should be used instead.

The summary table on pages 188–90 offers some advice about strengths and weaknesses of the different tools, although these are only generalizations.

Tools for Groups

The tools in this book should be used by groups of people. The use of some tools requires that all participants have prior knowledge of the tool at hand. For others, it is necessary only that the chairperson of the group knows the tool. An example of the latter is the use of brainstorming. It might be sufficient for the chairperson of the group to inform the others about the purpose and rules of brainstorming. However, a group where all participants have prior knowledge of and experience with brainstorming will most likely be far more efficient. If you know the tool you are using, you will focus more on the problem than the tool.

Working in groups has many benefits, but to work properly groups should have most of the following characteristics:

- An atmosphere of trust, openness, support, and honesty

- No fear of consequences when an individual shares something

- Participants who know one another

- Participants who take responsibility for the success of the team

- Participants who contribute to discussions and listen actively

- Participants who give useful feedback and accept feedback easily

- Participants who get their messages across

Problem Solving

Root Cause Analysis

Problem Understanding

Problem Cause Brainstorming

Problem Cause Data Collection

Problem Cause Data Analysis

Root Cause Identification

Root Cause Elimination

Solution Implementation

Tool Selection

Example Cases

Problem Solving

Root Cause
Analysis

Problem
Understanding

Problem Cause
Brainstorming

Problem Cause
Data Collection

Problem Cause
Data Analysis

Root Cause
Identification

Root Cause
Elimination

Solution
Implementation

Tool Selection

Example Cases

PROBLEM UNDERSTANDING
TOOL SELECTION

As you remember, problem understanding is made up of approaches that help get to the bottom of the problem you want to solve. This stage focuses on understanding the nature of the problem and is a preparatory step before starting the analysis. A flowchart for the problem understanding stage is shown below and explained on the following page.

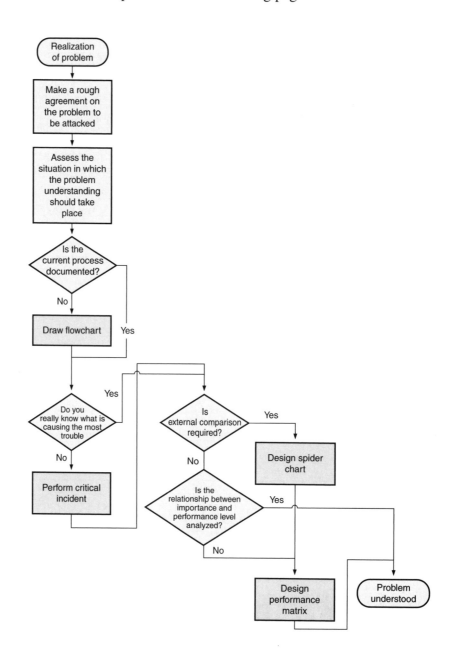

TOOL SELECTION FLOWCHART FOR PROBLEM UNDERSTANDING EXPLAINED

First, agree on the problem to be attacked. Then, assess the situation in which the problem understanding will occur and select a suitable approach. Typical considerations are pre-analysis problem understanding and how many people have been involved in debates about the problem so far.

Second, ask whether the process is already documented. If not, draw one or more flowcharts to depict the flow of activities in the process containing the problem.

Third, ask whether you really know what is causing the most trouble. If not, perform critical incident. The main purpose of the critical incident method is to understand what is really causing the most trouble in a problematic situation.

Fourth, ask whether any form of external comparison is required. If so, design a spider chart. Its main purpose is to give a graphic impression of how the performance of business processes or problem areas compare with other organizations.

Finally, ask whether the relationship between importance and performance level for the problem area or process should be analyzed. If not, the problem understanding stage is finished. If so, design a performance matrix to show the importance and current performance simultaneously to arrive at a sense of priority.

Problem Solving

Root Cause Analysis

Problem Understanding

Problem Cause Brainstorming

Problem Cause Data Collection

Problem Cause Data Analysis

Root Cause Identification

Root Cause Elimination

Solution Implementation

Tool Selection

Example Cases

Problem Solving

Root Cause
Analysis

Problem
Understanding

Problem Cause
Brainstorming

Problem Cause
Data Collection

Problem Cause
Data Analysis

Root Cause
Identification

Root Cause
Elimination

Solution
Implementation

Tool Selection

Example Cases

PROBLEM CAUSE BRAINSTORMING
TOOL SELECTION

Problem cause brainstorming is a collection of generic tools that can be applied at different stages in the analysis. Different ways of brainstorming can help you generate ideas about possible causes. The analysis is normally carried out in groups, so methods that help you arrive at consensus solutions are also useful. A flowchart for the problem cause brainstorming stage is shown below and explained on the next page. Note that problem cause brainstorming is not a streamlined process. One might, for instance, choose to use brainstorming and NGT together as one tool, and one or more of the tools might be used at other stages in the process.

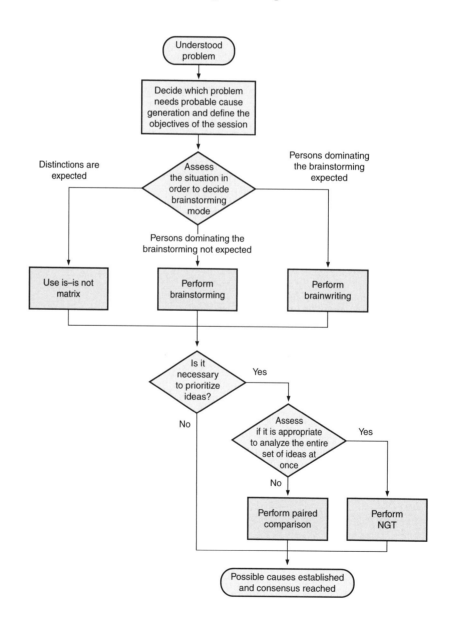

TOOL SELECTION FLOWCHART FOR PROBLEM CAUSE BRAINSTORMING EXPLAINED

First, decide which problem needs possible cause brainstorming and define the objective of the session. Typical applications are generating ideas about which problem to solve, possible causes for a problem, and possible solutions to a problem.

Next, assess the situation in which the possible cause brainstorming will occur and select an appropriate approach. Typical considerations are allowing everyone to participate properly, anonymity, complexity, and so forth, in addition to whether distinctions between what is part of the problem and what is not are expected. If there is a chance that any member might dominate the group, use brainwriting instead of brainstorming. If distinctions are foreseen, use the is–is not matrix.

After the brainstorming is completed, decide whether prioritization of the generated ideas is necessary. If not, the possible cause brainstorming and consensus stage is finished. If so, assess whether it is appropriate to analyze the entire set of ideas all at once. The purpose of this assessment is to select between the nominal group technique or paired comparisons. The main purpose of the nominal group technique is to facilitate a form of brainstorming in which all participants have the same vote when selecting solutions, while the idea behind paired comparison is that single decisions are easier to make than selecting among a large number of possibilities.

Problem Solving

Root Cause Analysis

Problem Understanding

Problem Cause Brainstorming

Problem Cause Data Collection

Problem Cause Data Analysis

Root Cause Identification

Root Cause Elimination

Solution Implementation

Tool Selection

Example Cases

Problem Solving

Root Cause
Analysis

Problem
Understanding

Problem Cause
Brainstorming

Problem Cause
Data Collection

Problem Cause
Data Analysis

Root Cause
Identification

Root Cause
Elimination

Solution
Implementation

Tool Selection

Example Cases

PROBLEM CAUSE DATA COLLECTION
TOOL SELECTION

Problem cause data collection is a set of generic tools and techniques that help render the data collection systematic, efficient, and effective. A flowchart for the problem cause data collection stage is shown below and explained on the following page.

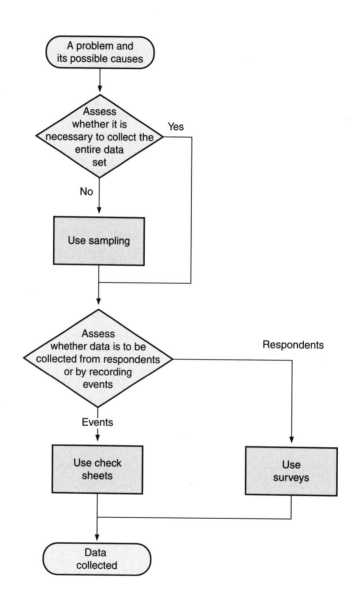

TOOL SELECTION FLOWCHART FOR PROBLEM CAUSE DATA COLLECTION EXPLAINED

Based on the outcome of the problem cause brainstorming stage, use a problem and its possible causes as the starting point of the problem cause data collection stage.

Next, assess whether it is necessary to collect data from the entire population. Typical considerations are the amount of data needed, the nature of the population, the costs involved, and so on. If using a smaller population is acceptable, use sampling. The main purpose of sampling is to allow drawing conclusions about a larger group based on a smaller sample, as long as you are aware of the sample's limitations.

Finally, assess whether you will collect data from respondents or by recording events that occur. In the former case, use surveys. In the latter, a check sheet is an appropriate tool. Surveys are used to collect data from different respondent groups while a check sheet is used to ensure that all data is registered correctly.

Problem Solving

Root Cause Analysis

Problem Understanding

Problem Cause Brainstorming

Problem Cause Data Collection

Problem Cause Data Analysis

Root Cause Identification

Root Cause Elimination

Solution Implementation

Tool Selection

Example Cases

Problem Solving

Root Cause
Analysis

Problem
Understanding

Problem Cause
Brainstorming

Problem Cause
Data Collection

Problem Cause
Data Analysis

Root Cause
Identification

Root Cause
Elimination

Solution
Implementation

Tool Selection

Example Cases

PROBLEM CAUSE DATA ANALYSIS
TOOL SELECTION

Problem cause data analysis is about making the most of all the data collected about the problem. When analyzing the same set of data from different angles, many different conclusions may emerge. Some of these might uncover the problem's causes, others not; thus it is important to have a number of data analysis tools available. A flowchart for the problem cause data analysis stage is shown below and explained on the following page.

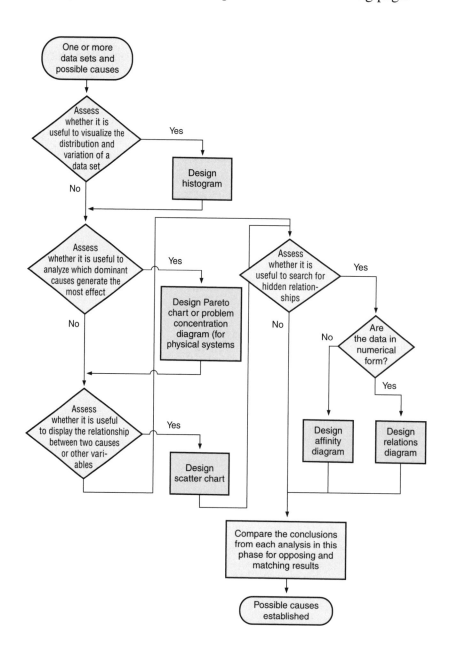

TOOL SELECTION FLOWCHART FOR PROBLEM CAUSE DATA ANALYSIS TOOL EXPLAINED

Based on the outcome of the problem cause data collection stage, use one or more data sets pertaining to the problem at hand and its possible causes as the starting point for the problem cause data analysis stage.

First, assess whether it is useful to visually display the distribution and variation of a data set. If so, design either a histogram or, in the case of a physical system where the location of problem occurrences is important, a problem concentration diagram.

Second, ask yourself whether it is useful to display the dominant causes that generate the most effects. If so, create a Pareto chart.

Third, determine whether it is useful to display the relationship between two causes or other variables. If so, create a scatter chart.

Fourth, assess whether it is useful to search for relationships among the variables and causes that might be hidden or obscure. If this is not useful, the problem cause data analysis stage is finished. If it could be useful, ask whether the data are in a numerical form or not. If they are, design a relations diagram. If not, use an affinity diagram instead.

The conclusions from each analysis at this stage should be compared for opposing or matching results.

The conclusions from the problem cause data analysis stage are then brought forward into the root cause identification stage.

Problem Solving
Root Cause Analysis
Problem Understanding
Problem Cause Brainstorming
Problem Cause Data Collection
Problem Cause Data Analysis
Root Cause Identification
Root Cause Elimination
Solution Implementation
Tool Selection
Example Cases

Problem Solving

Root Cause
Analysis

Problem
Understanding

Problem Cause
Brainstorming

Problem Cause
Data Collection

Problem Cause
Data Analysis

Root Cause
Identification

Root Cause
Elimination

Solution
Implementation

Tool Selection

Example Cases

ROOT CAUSE IDENTIFICATION
TOOL SELECTION

The root cause identification stage is at the heart of the roof cause analysis. As previously mentioned, root cause analysis is not one single approach; neither is this group of tools. It contains a few tools that combine to make up an in-depth analysis of the problem's root cause(s). A flowchart for the root cause identification stage is shown below and explained on the following page.

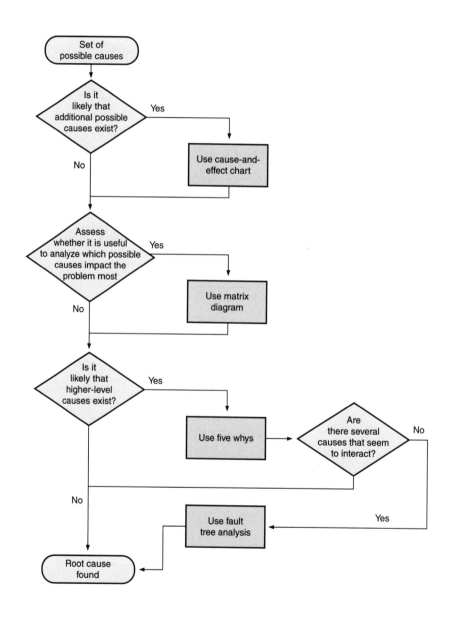

TOOL SELECTION FLOWCHART FOR ROOT CAUSE IDENTIFICATION EXPLAINED

From the outcome of the problem cause data analysis stage, a set of possible causes constitutes the starting point for the root cause identification stage.

First, ask, "Is it likely that there are additional possible causes to be found?" If the answer is yes—even a hesitant yes—run a cause-and-effect chart session.

Second, ask, "Is it useful to analyze which of the possible causes seem to impact the problem the most?" If yes, create a matrix diagram.

Third, ask, "Is it likely that there are higher-level causes of the problem, beyond those already identified?" Again, even a hesitant confirmation should lead to the application of the five whys tool.

Finally, check to determine if the conclusions from the root cause identification stage are true and relevant conclusions about the root cause of the problem being analyzed.

| Problem Solving |
| Root Cause Analysis |
| Problem Understanding |
| Problem Cause Brainstorming |
| Problem Cause Data Collection |
| Problem Cause Data Analysis |
| Root Cause Identification |
| Root Cause Elimination |
| Solution Implementation |
| **Tool Selection** |
| Example Cases |

ROOT CAUSE ELIMINATION
TOOL SELECTION

Root cause elimination is typically a creative task that can be difficult to outline as a streamlined process. We have, however, tried to sketch the rough steps of this phase, depicted in the flowchart below and explained on the following page.

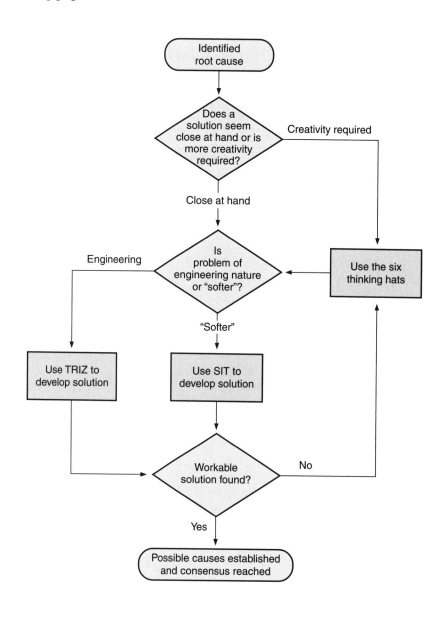

TOOL SELECTION FLOWCHART FOR ROOT CAUSE ELIMINATION EXPLAINED

Based on the outcome of the root cause identification stage, use the identified root cause as the starting point of the root cause elimination stage.

Consider whether there seem to be possible solutions "floating around"; that is, ideas that have been mentioned, similar problems that have been solved before, or solutions that can be purchased from suppliers. If not, it seems wise to start with a more creative session using the six thinking hats.

If a solution seems closer at hand, the next question is whether the problem is of a typical engineering type (that is, related to machinery, product details, and so on) or of a "softer" nature (that is, related to people, business processes, market issues, and so on). In the former case, TRIZ is a suitable tool; in the latter, SIT is the more obvious choice. However, this is not a black-and-white issue, as SIT can work well for engineering problems as well.

Finally, check whether a workable solution has been found. If not, the process should be repeated.

Problem Solving
Root Cause Analysis
Problem Understanding
Problem Cause Brainstorming
Problem Cause Data Collection
Problem Cause Data Analysis
Root Cause Identification
Root Cause Elimination
Solution Implementation
Tool Selection
Example Cases

Problem Solving

Root Cause
Analysis

Problem
Understanding

Problem Cause
Brainstorming

Problem Cause
Data Collection

Problem Cause
Data Analysis

Root Cause
Identification

Root Cause
Elimination

Solution
Implementation

Tool Selection

Example Cases

SOLUTION IMPLEMENTATION
TOOL SELECTION

Solution implementation is a difficult stage in an improvement project and requires leadership skills, psychological insight, and project management knowledge. Some tools also are available to help in creating a favorable change climate and planning the implementation project. A flowchart for the solution implementation stage is shown below and explained on the following page.

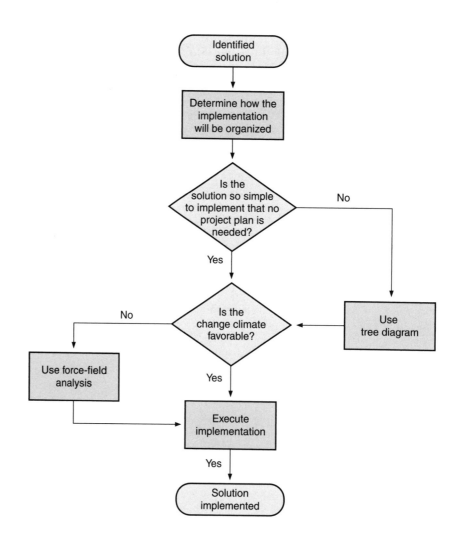

TOOL SELECTION FLOWCHART FOR SOLUTION IMPLEMENTATION EXPLAINED

Based on the outcome of the root cause elimination stage, use the devised solution as the starting point of the solution implementation stage.

First, start by determining how the implementation task should be organized: by the original improvement team, by a separate implementation team, or in the line organization.

Next, assess whether the implementation task seems so simple that a project plan is not required. Typical considerations are the number of activities, the number of people involved, the duration of the implementation job, and so on. If this is not the case, a tree diagram should be used to design such a plan.

Finally, assess whether the change climate is favorable or problems are foreseen in implementing the change. In the former case, proceed with executing the implementation. In the latter, use a force-field analysis to determine forces for and against the change before executing the implementation.

Problem Solving
Root Cause Analysis
Problem Understanding
Problem Cause Brainstorming
Problem Cause Data Collection
Problem Cause Data Analysis
Root Cause Identification
Root Cause Elimination
Solution Implementation
Tool Selection
Example Cases

TOOL SUMMARY

The following table summarizes some key aspects of the tools that have been presented in this book. When deciding which tool to use, refer to this table for guidance, but remember that the specific situation in which the tool will be used also impacts its suitability.

Stage/ Tool	Purpose	Strengths/ Advantages	Weaknesses/ Difficulties
Problem understanding			
Flowchart	Understand the flow of activities in a process	• Easy to use • Uses graphics	• Difficult to decide on the level of detail
Critical incident	Understand what are the most troublesome symptoms	• Allows everyone to participate • Generates many ideas	• Requires trust and openness
Spider chart	Compare performance with external references	• Easily understandable graphic presentation	• Difficult to obtain the necessary data
Performance matrix	Prioritize problems or symptoms to attack	• Leads to a structured analysis • Graphical approach	• Requires subjective assessments
Problem cause brainstorming			
Brainstorming	Generate as many ideas as possible	• Easy to use • Involves many people	• One/few persons can dominate • No anonymity is possible
Brainwriting	Generate as many ideas as possible	• Involves many people • Enables anonymity	• Can be less spontaneous than brainstorming
Is–is not matrix	Generate ideas about the problem, focusing especially on what does and does not characterize it	• Separates clearly between effects that do and don't occur • Allows seeing contracts/odd issues more clearly	• Can be difficult to come up with "is not" elements
Nominal group technique	Prioritize ideas	• Easy to use • Allows everyone equal vote	• Can be difficult to choose among many alternatives
Paired comparisons	Prioritize ideas	• Requires comparing only two and two alternatives instead of several at the same time	• With many alternatives, the exercise becomes infeasible due to too high a number of pairs

Continued

Continued

Stage/ Tool	Purpose	Strengths/ Advantages	Weaknesses/ Difficulties
Problem cause data collection			
Sampling	Gain a representative sample from a large population	• Minimizes the data collection effort	• Difficult to decide on the type of sampling and sample size • The sample may not be representative
Surveys	Collect data from respondents	• Allows collection of large amounts of data	• Good surveys are difficult to design • Often low response rate
Check sheet	Register data in a systematic fashion	• Easy to use • Ensures that all data are captured	• Data categories not specified may be overlooked
Problem cause data analysis			
Histogram	Portray data graphically	• Easy to see patterns • Uses graphics	• Difficult to identify classes
Pareto chart	Find the few elements causing most effects	• Striking graphics	• Multiple axes in the same chart
Scatter chart	Find relationships between two variables	• Easy to comprehend graphics	• Difficult to select the independent and dependent variable
Problem concentration diagram	Discover physical problem occurrences patterns	• Shows graphically where problems occur • Can be used to analyze data already collected, using check sheets for example	• Drawing a map that represents the real-life system well can be difficult
Relations diagram	Find relationships among many elements	• Provides a structured approach • Gives a clear graphic picture	• Relies on subjective assessments • The diagram could become quite complex
Affinity diagram	Find relationships otherwise not easily seen	• Can reveal hard-to-recognize relationships	• Requires creativity, patience, and previous experience • Less structured
Root cause identification			
Cause-and-effect chart	Generate and group problem causes	• Easy to use • Promotes structure *and* creativity	• One/few persons many dominate the exercise

Problem Solving

Root Cause Analysis

Problem Understanding

Problem Cause Brainstorming

Problem Cause Data Collection

Problem Cause Data Analysis

Root Cause Identification

Root Cause Elimination

Solution Implementation

Tool Selection

Example Cases

Continued

Stage/ Tool	Purpose	Strengths/ Advantages	Weaknesses/ Difficulties
Root cause identification continued			
Matrix diagram	Analyze causal relationships	• Provides structure to the analysis • Displays combined impact of factors	• Relies on subjective assessments • Some diagram types can be complex to use
Five whys	Identity chains of cause-and-effect	• Easy to use • Finds the root cause	• Requires some creativity and deep knowledge of the problem
Fault tree analysis	Graphically display branches of cause-and-effect relationships	• Creates insight into how causes interact • Can use results already produced using five whys	• In the case of many causes on many levels, the diagram can be difficult to construct and read
Root cause elimination			
The six thinking hats	Generate several solution ideas	• Forces people to take on different mind-sets • Easy to use	• Requires some practice to become effective • Rarely arrives at clear-cut conclusions
TRIZ	Find workable solutions, especially for engineering problems	• Is based on tabulated general solution principles • Is known to create good and creative solutions	• Can be difficult to apply well • Less suited for "softer" problems
SIT	Find creative and workable solutions	• Is based on templates that help the analysis • Is known to create good and creative solutions	• Can be difficult to apply well
Solution implementation			
Tree diagram	Design a project plan for the implementation of the solution	• Structures the activities of the implementation • Allows sequencing activities properly	• Becomes complex with many activities • Less suited for pure project planning than more advanced tools
Force-field analysis	Understanding the forces working for and against a change	• Illustrates the whole change climate in one diagram • Easy to use	• Can be difficult to assess the strength of the forces

11

Example Cases

Problem Solving

Root Cause Analysis

Problem Understanding

Problem Cause Brainstorming

Problem Cause Data Collection

Problem Cause Data Analysis

Root Cause Identification

Root Cause Elimination

Solution Implementation

Tool Selection

Example Cases

In the previous chapters, we have presented a number of tools for root cause analysis, guidelines for selecting them, and some examples of their use. In this chapter, we present two examples of how a selection of these tools have been applied in a concerted fashion in two companies: the travel agent Business Quality Travel and the manufacturer of plastic shopping bags Carry Me Home Shopping Bags.

Problem Solving

Root Cause
Analysis

Problem
Understanding

Problem Cause
Brainstorming

Problem Cause
Data Collection

Problem Cause
Data Analysis

Root Cause
Identification

Root Cause
Elimination

Solution
Implementation

Tool Selection

Example Cases

BUSINESS QUALITY TRAVEL

Business Quality Travel (BQT) is a medium-sized travel agency. BQT has 25 employees and a turnover of $30 million a year. The majority of BQT's employees are women between 25 and 40 years old. BQT has a rather flat organization with three levels: manager, group leader, and operator. BQT's core business is business travel but it also offers guidance for leisure trips. Although BQT is located in downtown Grand Peak, most customers prefer to order their trips by telephone. The number of trips ordered by e-mail and on the Internet has risen recently, but the numbers are still low. Trips can also be ordered by fax, but approximately 90 percent of the trips still are booked by phone. Often the traveler calls to order, but secretaries order about 20 percent of the trips.

Frame Agreements and Problems

BQT is trying to establish closer relationships with its key customers and has recently established frame agreements with nine large companies. The agreements state that BQT is the preferred and exclusive travel agent for these companies. In return, BQT provides substantial discounts on the tickets these companies buy. In addition, these companies have access to a dedicated hotline for ordering tickets. A group of BQT's employees work only with these key companies, of which one is a very large customer.

Lately, BQT has been experiencing some difficulties. Absenteeism due to illness among the employees has risen. The internal conflict level at BQT has also increased. Every other day, the manager spots indications of a poor working environment. The annual spring dinner for all employees had to be cancelled due to a low sign-up rate. The main problem, however, is that the manager has received complaints from customers regarding the service level at BQT. Often, it was impossible to get through on the phone to an operator, and the service provided (when they finally reached one) was not adequate. Some customers had even experienced rude comments from BQT's employees.

PROBLEM UNDERSTANDING AT BQT

The general manager arranged a meeting with a selected employee representative and they agreed that the company was facing a serious problem. They agreed to form a group to analyze the situation and find the root cause. The group consisted of the general manager, Elizabeth; the employee representative, John; a senior travel agent operator, Ann; and a junior operator, Deb. Among the group's first decisions were: a) to use the methodologies presented in this book to solve the problem, b) the problem might be related to the working environment in one way or another, and c) the group would meet frequently and keep an open mind during the process. Ann was selected as chairperson of the group and John was selected as the group's secretary.

Flowchart and Critical Incident

As the current process was not properly documented, the first thing the group had to do was to draw a flowchart to document the current process. The flowchart is shown on the following page.

The next question for the group was whether they really knew what was causing the most trouble. No one in the group could give a definite answer to this question, and thus they performed a critical incident analysis. The results showed that many operators:

- Did not know how to handle requests

- Had no time for breaks

- Could not find data in the computer-based system

- Were handling only complex travel routes

- Got headaches

- Did not have time to get back to customers

- Worked too much overtime

- Received insufficient information from customers

Problem Solving

Root Cause Analysis

Problem Understanding

Problem Cause Brainstorming

Problem Cause Data Collection

Problem Cause Data Analysis

Root Cause Identification

Root Cause Elimination

Solution Implementation

Tool Selection

Example Cases

Problem Solving

Root Cause
Analysis

Problem
Understanding

Problem Cause
Brainstorming

Problem Cause
Data Collection

Problem Cause
Data Analysis

Root Cause
Identification

Root Cause
Elimination

Solution
Implementation

Tool Selection

Example Cases

BQT FLOWCHART

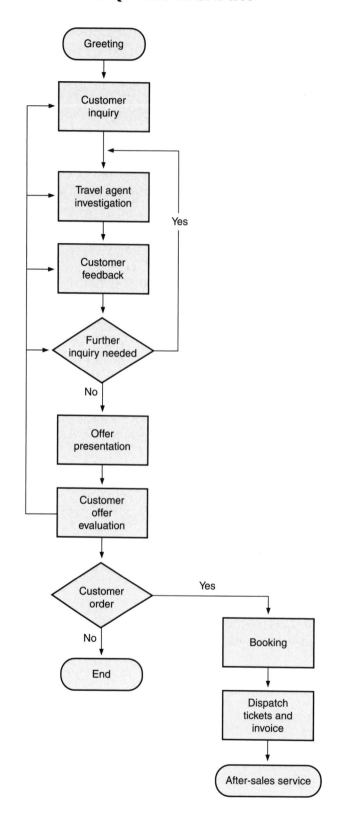

BQT PERFORMANCE MATRIX

The next question the group discussed was whether any type of external comparison could be useful. The manager suggested finding out whether other travel agents have similar problems, and the group agreed that this might be a good idea. The manager talked with managers of other travel agencies he knew, and it seemed that about half of them were experiencing similar difficulties, but none of the managers knew exactly why. The types of difficulties varied somewhat from agency to agency, and some were considering analyzing the situation.

In the end, the team completed the problem understanding stage by designing a performance matrix, as shown below. Based on the matrix, they concluded that the main problem seemed to be the poor overall availability of BQT's operators to its customers.

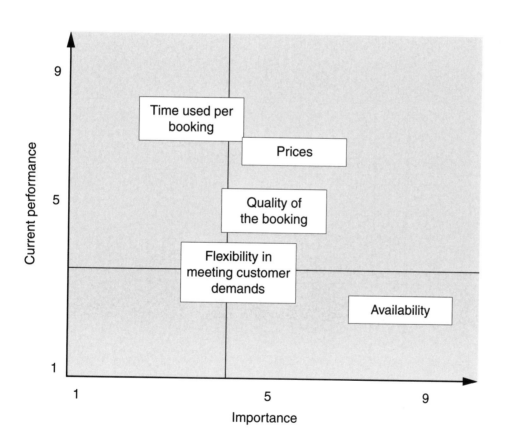

Problem Solving

Root Cause Analysis

Problem Understanding

Problem Cause Brainstorming

Problem Cause Data Collection

Problem Cause Data Analysis

Root Cause Identification

Root Cause Elimination

Solution Implementation

Tool Selection

Example Cases

Problem Solving

Root Cause Analysis

Problem Understanding

Problem Cause Brainstorming

Problem Cause Data Collection

Problem Cause Data Analysis

Root Cause Identification

Root Cause Elimination

Solution Implementation

Tool Selection

Example Cases

PROBLEM CAUSE BRAINSTORMING AT BQT

At the next meeting of the root cause analysis group, the team performed possible cause brainstorming.

To decide whether to use brainstorming or brainwriting, each member received a piece of paper on which they wrote S or W. It was agreed that if anyone wrote W, brainwriting would be applied.

The results were three S's and one W, and the results of the brainwriting are shown below.

Results from the Brainwriting

The assumed main problem was determined to be:

- Poor operator availability to customers

Proposed possible causes included:

- Low capacity

- Frequent leaves of absence

- Customers not knowing what they want, causing the booking to take a long time

- Not enough knowledge to handle requests

- New technology

- Interface with the booking system is slow

- No incentives to work harder

- Increased percentage of customers wanting complex travel routes

PROBLEM CAUSE DATA COLLECTION AT BQT

After an initial assessment, the group concluded that the amount of data available concerning the problem and its causes was very limited. Ann argued that they should use some kind of check sheet to collect data from the processes. Elizabeth agreed, while John and Deb felt it would be appropriate to send a survey to the employees. After a heated discussion, Deb suggested they use both; the others agreed. The check sheet was designed to collect data on the time the operators spent on each task in the booking process. The survey was designed to collect the views the travel agents had on the suggested possible causes. The data was collected over a one-week period.

Problem Solving
Root Cause Analysis
Problem Understanding
Problem Cause Brainstorming
Problem Cause Data Collection
Problem Cause Data Analysis
Root Cause Identification
Root Cause Elimination
Solution Implementation
Tool Selection
Example Cases

Questions Asked in the Survey

Dear employee,

Our company has been experiencing some problems lately, and a group has been established to find the root cause of these problems. So far we have established that the major problem is the availability of BQT's employees to its customers. Based on this assumption, we are conducting this small survey. Please answer each question by checking the appropriate box.

On a scale from 1 (poor) to 5 (good), how do you assess our availability?

❑   ❑   ❑   ❑   ❑
1   2   3   4   5

Which of the following items contributes most to the lack of availability?

❑   1   Low capacity

❑   2   Frequent leaves of absence

❑   3   Customers not knowing what they want, causing booking to take a long time

❑   4   Not enough knowledge to handle requests

❑   5   New technology

❑   6   Interface with the booking system is slow

❑   7   No incentives to work hard

❑   8   Percentage of customers wanting complex travel routes increasing

Problem Solving

Root Cause
Analysis

Problem
Understanding

Problem Cause
Brainstorming

Problem Cause
Data Collection

Problem Cause
Data Analysis

Root Cause
Identification

Root Cause
Elimination

Solution
Implementation

Tool Selection

Example Cases

PROBLEM CAUSE DATA ANALYSIS AT BQT

The check sheet data on time consumption in the booking process revealed very few interesting findings. For the survey data on the employees' beliefs as to what caused the poor availability, a simple histogram-like chart was produced to visualize the response distribution, as shown below.

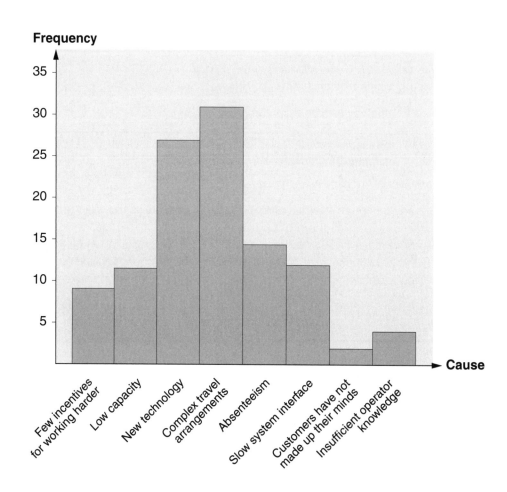

From the chart, two obvious candidates stood out in terms of being important problem causes, namely:

- New technology and problems related to its use

- A movement toward more complex travel arrangements, as many customers were now booking simple trips themselves via the Internet

ROOT CAUSE IDENTIFICATION AT BQT

After initially getting excited about finding the apparent solutions to the problems' causes, the team decided that perhaps their work was not yet over. When pondering these two causes, they found that there probably were additional higher-level causes and decided to employ the five whys approach as a final step in the investigation. The result, after four whys, is shown below:

Low operator availability

Why? New technology and complex travel arrangements

    Why? Pressure for efficiency, and customers booking simpler trips directly from the airlines

        Why? Low margins on tickets and the airlines often offer better discounts

            Why? The ticket commission from the airlines has been reduced significantly over the last two years

---

The Root Cause

Even if the analysis could be brought no further than four whys, the team felt absolutely certain that they had really uncovered the true root cause of the problem. When they suddenly realized that many of the problems were in fact caused, directly or indirectly, by the dramatic cuts in ticket commissions from the airlines, the pieces finally fell into place.

These cuts had produced immense pressure to make up for the lost income. This had produced a very stressful climate, both at BQT and many other travel agencies, which in turn had led to the introduction of new technologies. As customers started to approach the travel agents only when they had questions about more complex trips, each inquiry took longer. All in all, this caused the operators to spend more time on the phone with clients, while earning less per call. This materialized into a problem visible to the customers; that is, that it was difficult to get through to an operator.

Problem Solving

Root Cause Analysis

Problem Understanding

Problem Cause Brainstorming

Problem Cause Data Collection

Problem Cause Data Analysis

Root Cause Identification

Root Cause Elimination

Solution Implementation

Tool Selection

Example Cases

Problem Solving
Root Cause Analysis
Problem Understanding
Problem Cause Brainstorming
Problem Cause Data Collection
Problem Cause Data Analysis
Root Cause Identification
Root Cause Elimination
Solution Implementation
Tool Selection
Example Cases

ROOT CAUSE ELIMINATION AT BQT

The reduction of ticket commissions from the airlines had now been identified as the root cause. The improvement group was satisfied about having found the root cause, but they had a hard time figuring out how to eliminate it. After first having tried a nonsystematic approach with no luck, the group decided to use the six thinking hats. For this session, three more employees were included in the group in order to enhance the output from the session. The improvement group was given a briefing in the use of the tool, and they agreed to use the tool in a thorough manner.

Solutions Devised

The group was able to apply the concept of the six thinking hats successfully. The following solution emerged:

As BQT is not in a position that enables it to dictate ticket commissions from the airlines, the solution should focus on how BQT could have an acceptable profit margin. This could be done by differentiating the product, thus offering a value-adding service customers will pay for. The team found that BQT had special expertise in travel to Europe, and especially to Italy and France. If BQT could promote itself as the leading business travel agency for bringing American businesses closer to these markets, it would be an attractive partner. BQT could also develop a close relationship with local interpreters and business facilitators, which could enhance business trips to the region.

Developing this idea further, a range of additional services could be included, for example, arranging site visits to European companies, facilitating conferences or seminars, arranging leisure programs for accompanying persons, and so on. Doing a quick market check with some potential customers, it was soon confirmed that companies would be willing to pay good money for such a comprehensive travel arrangement service.

ROOT CAUSE ELIMINATION AT BQT

Having found a suitable solution, BQT developed an implementation plan. The plan included setting up frame agreements with partners in France and Italy, both hotels and industrial companies. Product development was also an important task, converting the loose ideas into a set of services with a price structure. New informational materials had to be developed, and the new services had to be marketed. The plan was executed in several iterations as BQT could not change its business structure over night. The focus was on creating acceptance for the required changes and a favorable climate for the implementation for all major stakeholders, especially BQT's customers and employees. In order to enhance the acceptance of the solution, a force-field analysis was performed. The former frustration of the employees helped motivate them for the improvement process.

Patience

BQT succeeded in finding the root cause and eliminating it. A major reason for this was their use of the structured approach explained in this book. Another major reason was the true involvement of the employees and management in the process. To maintain such momentum is often a great challenge, especially in the latter phases of the process. All involved should be patient.

Problem Solving

Root Cause Analysis

Problem Understanding

Problem Cause Brainstorming

Problem Cause Data Collection

Problem Cause Data Analysis

Root Cause Identification

Root Cause Elimination

Solution Implementation

Tool Selection

Example Cases

Problem Solving

Root Cause
Analysis

Problem
Understanding

Problem Cause
Brainstorming

Problem Cause
Data Collection

Problem Cause
Data Analysis

Root Cause
Identification

Root Cause
Elimination

Solution
Implementation

Tool Selection

Example Cases

CARRY ME HOME SHOPPING BAGS

Carry Me Home Shopping Bags (CMHSB) is a small group of five manufacturing units spread across the Benelux countries of Belgium, the Netherlands, and Luxembourg. The group is built around one main product, plastic shopping bags. These come in a variety of sizes and designs, thus making them suitable for anything from small, specialized shops to large grocery store chains, the latter accounting for about 60 percent of their turnover. In this example, we will concentrate on one of these manufacturing sites. This is a "lean" unit with 27 employees: one managing director, two multipurpose managers, and three shifts of eight factory operators. The annual turnover is about $ 8.1 million and there is great pressure on each unit to stay competitive, with the threat of being closed down and production transferred to one of the others ever present.

The Manufacturing Process

Very roughly, bags are made through a process of four steps:

- Extrusion of plastic granulate into film

- Printing of the bags with company logos, text, and so on

- Conversion, consisting of cutting the film into bags and welding the bags' seams

- Packaging into cardboard boxes ready for shipping

The entire process is heavily automated, requiring only eight operators to run a setup of three plastic film extruders and three integrated lines for printing, conversion, and packaging.

The extruded film comes out of the machine as a tube that is laid flat and rolled up for intermediate storage. The roll is three times the width of a finished bag, approximately 59 inches (150 cm).

The remaining three steps run in-line from film on a roll all the way to sets of 50 folded bags packed 20 sets in each cardboard box. The speed of this line is about 110 yards per minute (150 meters per minute), leaving little room for error in equipment or material.

PROBLEM UNDERSTANDING AND PROBLEM CAUSE BRAINSTORMING AT CMHSB

In general, production ran smoothly with a unit per hour count among the highest in the group. Intermittently, however, the conversion line would stop due to problems with the material flow through the machines. The film would break or jam, the welding became uneven, and so on. With each stop, cleaning up and restarting could take anywhere from two minutes up to three hours, lowering productivity dramatically. Despite much effort to adjust different process parameters, the problem just would not go away. For weeks, everything would run nicely, then out of nowhere the line would stop and continue being difficult until suddenly things started to work again. While it came as a relief each time things unexpectedly worked again, it left everyone none the wiser and just as vulnerable for a recurrence.

Flowcharting and Brute Force in the Beginning

After adjusting every possible process parameter, changing parts, and making sure the raw material was stable, the entire staff was truly perplexed about the cause of the difficulties. Having been one of the very first companies in the country to start plastic manufacturing back in 1965, few were around with more expertise so there was really no one to call for help.

Being at first more or less unaware of more systematic problem-solving techniques, operators and managers started brainstorming about possible causes that had been overlooked. A type of flowchart, in the form of a layout diagram for the manufacturing process, was constructed and studied closely (see next page). One idea that quickly came to mind was compatibility problems between the extruder and the conversion line, meaning that rolls from one extruder might cause problems in one conversion line but not on the other two.

To test the hypothesis, an effort was made to determine which extruder–conversion line combination was used when problems occurred. This was achieved by marking each roll of plastic film with the extruder number and simply recording the extruder number when the roll messed up the line.

To everyone's surprise, there were no patterns to be seen. Apparently total random combinations caused the problems.

Problem Solving

Root Cause Analysis

Problem Understanding

Problem Cause Brainstorming

Problem Cause Data Collection

Problem Cause Data Analysis

Root Cause Identification

Root Cause Elimination

Solution Implementation

Tool Selection

Example Cases

Problem Solving

Root Cause
Analysis

Problem
Understanding

Problem Cause
Brainstorming

Problem Cause
Data Collection

Problem Cause
Data Analysis

Root Cause
Identification

Root Cause
Elimination

Solution
Implementation

Tool Selection

Example Cases

CMHSB LAYOUT FLOWCHART

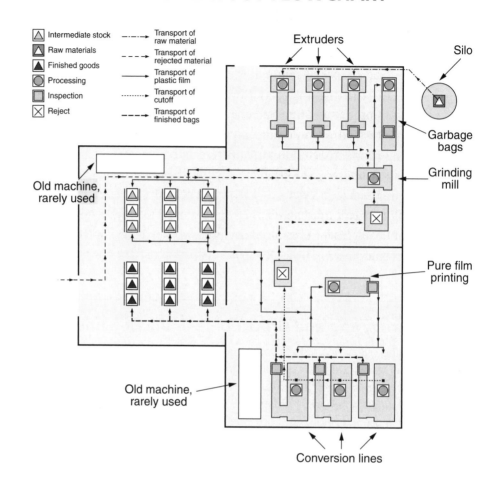

PROBLEM CAUSE DATA COLLECTION AT CMHSB

Getting nowhere with the approach of combining certain machines, the company realized that a more systematic line of attack had to be devised. As it seemed clear that there was something about the film that caused the conversion lines to stop, more data was required. The specifications for the film included a thickness of 35 μ (1 μ = 1 thousand of a millimeter), which was the main parameter that could possibly vary. All of the rolls of film had the right total weight, but that did not preclude thickness variation across a roll. Thus, it was decided to collect thickness data, using sampling to minimize the number of tests to be taken, and check sheets to record the data. To capture all possible variation, samples were to be taken longitudinally, that is, from different places along the length of the film, as well as across the width of the film roll.

| Problem Solving |
| Root Cause Analysis |
| Problem Understanding |
| Problem Cause Brainstorming |
| Problem Cause Data Collection |
| Problem Cause Data Analysis |
| Root Cause Identification |
| Root Cause Elimination |
| Solution Implementation |
| Tool Selection |
| **Example Cases** |

Data Collection

To identify problem causes, the sampling strategy defined was to take samples from rolls used when machines stopped. When such a bad roll came up, it was pulled out of production and replaced by a new one. From each roll that were removed, "strips" of 22 samples were taken as shown below: 11 from the visible front upper side of the film tube and 11 from the invisible underside.

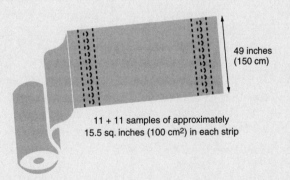

49 inches (150 cm)

11 + 11 samples of approximately 15.5 sq. inches (100 cm2) in each strip

For each strip, the weight of the 22 samples was measured, and, assuming a homogenous thickness across the circular sample, the thickness was calculated. The thickness data were then entered into a check sheet, one for each roll of film. A simplified version of the check sheet is shown on the upper half of the next page.

Problem Solving

Root Cause
Analysis

Problem
Understanding

Problem Cause
Brainstorming

Problem Cause
Data Collection

Problem Cause
Data Analysis

Root Cause
Identification

Root Cause
Elimination

Solution
Implementation

Tool Selection

Example Cases

PROBLEM CAUSE DATA ANALYSIS
AT CMHSB

Having collected data this way for a period of two months, plus taking samples from approximately 40 bad rolls stored during the last year, 590 strips (of 22 samples each) from 59 rolls had been recorded. These data were analyzed, partly by calculating some key statistical parameters (averages and standard deviation) and partly by using a histogram to portray thickness profiles across the width of the film.

Extruder #:												Date:										
											Sample #											
Strip #	1	2	3	4	5	6	7	8	9	10	11	12	13	14	15	16	17	18	19	20	21	22
1																						
2																						
3																						
n																						

Data Collection Results

The numbers below show weight data for one 22-sample strip, in milligrams (mg):

Extruder #:												Date:										
											Sample #											
Strip #	1	2	3	4	5	6	7	8	9	10	11	12	13	14	15	16	17	18	19	20	21	22
1	38	38	35	38	39	35	35	46	43	40	40	38	37	37	34	35	38	37	37	34	37	37

For this strip, the key statistical parameters were:

- Average weight 37.7 mg
- Average thickness 39.7 μ
- Standard deviation 2.84 mg

Comparing this with a strip from a good roll that ran without problems, there were clear deviations:

- Average weight 37.2 mg.
- Average thickness 39.3 μ.
- Standard deviation 1.31 mg.

Looking further into the differences between good and bad rolls, it soon became clear that good rolls averaged from 0.5 to 1.5 in standard deviation, with bad ones above 2.0.

PROBLEM CAUSE DATA ANALYSIS

Having identified a threshold value of 2.0 mg of standard deviation, a procedure was implemented where a sample strip was taken from every roll extruded. Rolls of standard deviation higher than 2.0 were simply deemed waste, ground and reused as raw material. This quickly eliminated most of the conversion line stops, but still the root cause of the film thickness variation had not been found. And although production ran better, the new procedure incurred extra costs in testing each roll and waste film that had to be reused.

To further the analysis, the thickness variation had to be understood better. It seemed clear that a histogram could be useful. By making bars represent each of the 22 samples, one histogram is generated per strip. The chart below is an example of such a histogram.

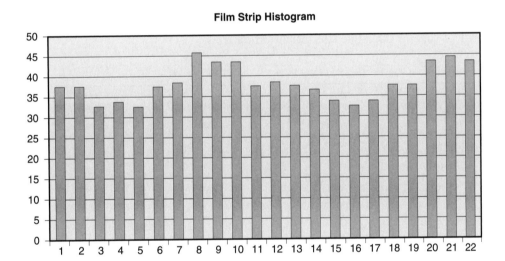

Problem Solving

Root Cause Analysis

Problem Understanding

Problem Cause Brainstorming

Problem Cause Data Collection

Problem Cause Data Analysis

Root Cause Identification

Root Cause Elimination

Solution Implementation

Tool Selection

Example Cases

ROOT CAUSE IDENTIFICATION AT CMHSB

Examining the histograms, a pattern emerged: two "peaks" of higher thickness and two "valleys" of lower thickness for each strip from bad rolls. As the film is a flattened tube, this meant that two opposing areas of the tube were thicker and two opposing areas thinner, as shown below.

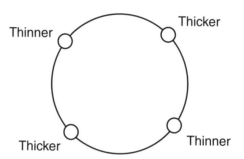

The question quickly became: in the extrusion machine, what were there four of that could cause this variation pattern?

The Root Cause

Studying the extruders, the obvious element appearing in a multiple of four was the frame supporting the film tube and keeping it in a circular shape. As shown in the pictures on the next page, the heated plastic is extruded through a tool (❷ in the upper picture). Air is blown through the inside of the extruded film tube, both to "inflate" it to its shape and to cool it. To stop the tube from expanding too much and to give it the circular shape, a supporting frame (❸ in the upper picture) is placed above the extrusion tool.

As the lower picture tries to show in more detail, the supporting frame consists of four arced steel rods with balls thread onto them (much like an abacus). Together, these four rods form a closed circle. However, depending on the diameter of the tube being extruded, the diameter of the frame can be adjusted inward or outward. Looking at the geometry of the supporting frame, one could quite easily see that it forms a perfect circle at a medium diameter, but at lower and higher diameters exhibits four irregularities, matching the thickness variation patterns observed.

The theory explaining this was that in these four areas the film was stretched a little more than elsewhere. Thus, minor cooling variation would occur, in turn introducing thickness variation.

CMHSB EXTRUDER PICTURES

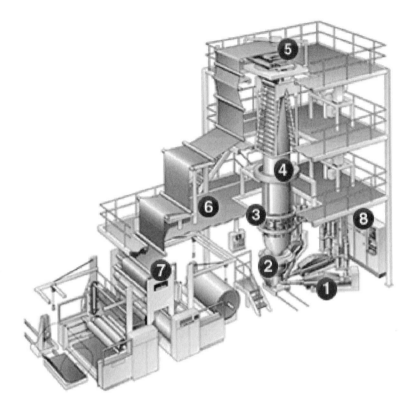

Problem Solving

Root Cause Analysis

Problem Understanding

Problem Cause Brainstorming

Problem Cause Data Collection

Problem Cause Data Analysis

Root Cause Identification

Root Cause Elimination

Solution Implementation

Tool Selection

Example Cases

Problem Solving

Root Cause Analysis

Problem Understanding

Problem Cause Brainstorming

Problem Cause Data Collection

Problem Cause Data Analysis

Root Cause Identification

Root Cause Elimination

Solution Implementation

Tool Selection

Example Cases

ROOT CAUSE ELIMINATION AT CMHSB

To solve the problem, the supporting frame was adjusted to form the perfect circle at the diameter used as much as 85 percent of the time. This should eliminate the root cause and enable the company to use every film roll.

Confidence in the solution was so great, even the procedure of testing all rolls was suspended before production resumed after the adjustment. Equally great was the surprise when exactly the same problems occurred shortly thereafter!

Intermediate-Level Cause Eliminated

Having had time to digest the disappointment and assess the situation again, new measurements showed that the number of bad rolls had been slightly reduced. Adjusting the supporting frame had obviously helped reduce the cooling variation somewhat. Still, this was apparently only an intermediate-level cause and not the true root cause, proving again that root cause analysis often involves several iterations.

ROOT CAUSE IDENTIFICATION, SECOND ITERATION

Realizing that the root cause hierarchy of this problem was more complex than first anticipated, a five whys approach seemed appropriate. A small team of people from different areas of the company convened to undertake the analysis. The data already collected, along with the analyses performed so far, were reviewed, leading to the following five whys outline:

> **Conversion line stops intermittently**

Why? Some bad rolls of film appear

> *Why?* Thickness variation across film width

> > *Why?* Uneven cooling of film during extrusion

> > > *Why?* Cooling pipe moved out of position

> > > > *Why?* Operators turn pipe a little each time when cleaning off excess plastic at startup

Five Whys Analysis

During the analysis, it became clear that one of the operators knew about this problem and assumed that everyone else did as well. What happened was that each time a new extrusion run was started, excess plastic had to be cleaned off around the extrusion tool. When doing so in a circular motion around the tool, the cooling pipe leading air upward typically would be turned a quarter or a half turn, on fine threads. After a few such "treatments," the pipe would be lifted so much that the cooling-air flow would change dramatically. As the drawing below shows, the cooling air is channeled through a slit formed between two cones placed one inside the other, thus sending the air out in an upward direction. Screwing the inner part up too high, air instead flows directly outward. When this happens, four ribs holding the pipe together at the slit become exposed and obstruct the air flow. It didn't take much analysis to see that these ribs matched the four points of thickness variation. The one operator aware of the cooling pipe problem would regularly adjust it back down. None of the other operators ever did, thus frequently allowing it to reach this position until the one aware operator again worked the machine and readjusted it.

Sidebar navigation:
- Problem Solving
- Root Cause Analysis
- Problem Understanding
- Problem Cause Brainstorming
- Problem Cause Data Collection
- Problem Cause Data Analysis
- Root Cause Identification
- Root Cause Elimination
- Solution Implementation
- Tool Selection
- **Example Cases**

Problem Solving

Root Cause
Analysis

Problem
Understanding

Problem Cause
Brainstorming

Problem Cause
Data Collection

Problem Cause
Data Analysis

Root Cause
Identification

Root Cause
Elimination

Solution
Implementation

Tool Selection

Example Cases

ROOT CAUSE ELIMINATION, SECOND ITERATION

After this epiphany, the company felt confident that the true root cause had been found. Eliminating it would thus be a question of making sure that the cooling pipe would not be raised so high that cooling was disrupted. There would probably be several possible ways of preventing this, and it was decided to use the approach of six thinking hats to reach a solution.

The managing director, one of the other managers, and four operators were assigned the various hats. Finding one or more solutions to the cooling pipe problem was defined as the main purpose of the session. After a couple of hours, several workable solutions seemed indeed to have emerged.

Solutions Devised

Having applied the concept of the six thinking hats successfully, two primary solutions stood out:

- Implementing a fixed routine of checking the position of the cooling pipe every morning

- Installing a locking pin on the cooling pipe that would have to be removed before any adjustment could be made to the pipe

A new routine would probably work quite well, but still held potential for human error. If the locking pin could be designed, it would be a foolproof solution. Thus, while work was started to design such a pin, a new routine of inspection was temporarily implemented.

SOLUTION IMPLEMENTATION AT CMHSB

A small team of operators, with assistance from the extrusion machine supplier, set out to find an easy way of installing the locking pin. It turned out to be quite easy: by simply drilling a small hole through the threaded area of the pipe and the base, and cutting threads through the length of the hole, a small locking screw could be mounted, keeping the pipe firmly in place.

Should there be a need to loosen the pipe for adjustment, cleaning, or servicing, the locking screw is easily removed to allow rotation of the pipe.

"Change Management"

Actually implementing the new solution was thus purely a matter of making the required technical changes to the three extrusion machines. There was no need to create a receptive change climate or assess forces opposing the change.

Shortly after implementing the locking screw on all three extruders, further film thickness measurements showed dramatic improvements, with much more consistent thickness. The number of bad rolls has been reduced by 90 percent and the cost savings have been estimated at about $100,000 annually.

Problem Solving

Root Cause Analysis

Problem Understanding

Problem Cause Brainstorming

Problem Cause Data Collection

Problem Cause Data Analysis

Root Cause Identification

Root Cause Elimination

Solution Implementation

Tool Selection

Example Cases

Further Reading and Additional Resources

This section contains an overview of the literature dealing with root cause analysis as a whole or subtopics of root cause analysis. Some deal with the topic differently than we have or deal with it in more detail. You will also find a guide to additional software resources that might be useful during analysis.

FURTHER READING

This list includes some suggested reading materials that treat the tools presented in this book (as well as others) in more detail.

Ammerman, Max. *The Root Cause Analysis Handbook: A Simplified Approach to Identifying, Correcting, and Reporting Workplace Errors*, New York: Quality Resources, 1998.

Altshuller, Genrich S., translated by Lev Shulyak and Steven Rodman. *40 Principles: TRIZ Keys to Technical Innovation*. Worchester, MA: Technical Innovation Center, 1997.

De Bono, Edward. *Six Thinking Hats*. Boston: Little, Brown, & Co., 1985.

Eastman Kodak Company *Quality Leadership Process Guidebook*. Rochester, NY: Eastman Kodak Co., 1990.

Fellers, Gary. *The Deming Vision SPC/TQM for Administrators*. Milwaukee: ASQC Quality Press, 1992.

Gitlow, Howard, Alan Oppenheim, and Rosa Oppenheim. *Quality Management: Tools and Methods for Improvement*. Burr Ridge, IL: Irwin, 1995.

Goldenberg, Jacob, and David Mazursky. *Creativity in Product Innovation*. Cambridge, MA: Cambridge University Press, 2002.

Lawlor, Alan. *Productivity Improvement Manual*. Aldershot, England: Gower, 1985.

Mizuno, Shigeru (editor). *Management for Quality Improvement: The 7 New QC Tools*. Cambridge, MA: Productivity Press, 1988.

Roberts, Lon. *SPC for Right-Brain Thinkers: Process Control for Non-Statisticians.* Milwaukee: ASQ Quality Press, 2005.

Scholtes, Peter R. *The Team Handbook: How to Use Teams to Improve Quality.* Madison, WI: Joiner, 1988.

Straker, David. *A Toolbook for Quality Improvement and Problem Solving.* London: Prentice-Hall, 1995.

Swanson, Roger C. *The Quality Improvement Handbook: Team Guide to Tools and Techniques.* London: Kogan Page, 1995.

Wilson, Paul F. *Root Cause Analysis Workbook.* Milwaukee: American Society for Quality, 1992.

Wilson, Paul F., Larry D. Dell, and Gaylord F. Anderson. *Root Cause Analysis: A Tool for Total Quality Management.* Milwaukee: American Society for Quality, 1993.

ADDITIONAL RESOURCES

Software tools that may be useful at different stages in root cause analysis are listed below. Since this book is not an advertising channel for different suppliers' software, no descriptions have been given. Essential information such as Web addresses, company addresses, and so on, is provided, but for some of the products, the list is not complete. In addition, it should be noted that the information listed will not be accurate indefinitely.

Microsoft Office Visio® 2003, http://office.microsoft.com/en-us/FX010857981033.aspx.
Microsoft Corporation, One Microsoft Way, Redmond, WA 98052, USA
Telephone: 425-882-8080
Fax: 425-706-7329

iGrafx® FlowCharter™, http://www.igrafx.com/products/flowcharter/index.html
iGrafx Inc., 7585 SW Mohawk, Tualatin, OR 97062, USA
Telephone: 503-692-8162
Fax: 503-691-2451

The Memory Jogger Software, http://www.goalqpc.com/
GOAL/QPC, 12B Manor Parkway, Suite 3, Salem, NH 03079-2862, USA
Telephone: 603-890-8800
Fax: 603-870-9122
E-mail: service@goalqpc.com

Statgraphics Centurion, http://www.statgraphics.com/
StatPoint, Inc., 2325 Dulles Corner Boulevard, Suite 500, Herndon, Virginia 20171, USA
Telephone: 540-364-0420
Fax: 540-364-0421
E-mail: info@statgraphics.com

SAS software, http://www.sas.com/sashome.html
SAS Institute Inc., SAS Campus Drive, Cary, NC 27513-2414, USA
Telephone: 919-677-8000
Fax: 919-677-4444

AutoCad, http://www.autodesk.com/
Autodesk, Inc., 111 McInnis Parkway, San Rafael, CA 94903, USA
Telephone: 415-507-5000
Fax: 415-507-5100

CADKEY, http://www.kubotekusa.com/products/cadkey/
Kubotek USA, Inc., 100 Locke Drive, Marlborough, MA 01752, USA
Telephone: 508-229-2020
Fax: 508-229-2121

ParaMind, http://www.paramind.net/
ParaMind Software, P.O. Box 27401, Seattle, WA 98125-2401, USA
E-mail: paramind@paramind.net

Index